DATE DUE

LIFE ISSUES

DROPPING OUT

Victoria Sherrow

BENCHMARK BOOKS

MARSHALL CAVENDISH

NEW YORK

Published by Marshall Cavendish Corporation
99 White Plains Road
Tarrytown, NY 10591
USA

© 1996 Marshall Cavendish Corporation

All rights reserved. No part of this book may be reproduced or utilized in any form or by any means electronic or mechanical, including photocopying, recording, or by any information storage and retrieval system, without permission from the copyright holders.

Library of Congress Cataloging-in-Publication Data

Sherrow, Victoria.
    Dropping out / Victoria Sherrow.
      p. cm. — (Life issues)
    Includes bibliographical references and index.
    Summary: Discusses some of the reasons for and consequences of not finishing high school, including poor study skills, learning disabilities, family problems, and violence.
    ISBN 0-7614-0018-4 (lib. bdg.)
    1. Dropouts—United States—Juvenile literature. [1. Dropouts. 2. High schools. 3. Schools.] I. Title. II. Series.
LC143.S44 1996
371.2'913'0973—dc20
                            95-11186
                            CIP
                            AC

Produced by Jacquerie Productions

Printed and bound in the United States of America

Photographic Note
Several persons depicted in this book are photographic models; their appearance in these photographs is solely to dramatize some of the situations and choices facing readers of the Life Issues series.

Photo Credits
Hazel Hankin: p. 58
Impact Visuals: p. 8 (Donna Binder); 14, 46, 83 (Dan Habib); 24 (Donna DeCesare); 27 (Dick Doughty);
    39, 77 (Harvey Finkle); 40 (Jeff Perkell); 42 (Tom McKitterick); 52 (Jeffry Scott); 62 (Catherine Smith);
    70, 75 (Jim West)
Ed Kashi: p. 34, 47
Richard Levine: p. 48
Photo Edit: p. 11 (Billy E. Barnes)
The Picture Cube: p. 4, 23, 64 (Robert Finken); 6 (Spencer Grant); 16 (Nancy Sheehan); 19 (Robert W. Ginn);
    29 (Jon Goell); 32 (John Coletti); 37, 50, 60 (Jeff Greenberg); 45, 81, 88 (Frank Siteman); 55 (J. Berndt);
    66, 68 (Tom McCarthy); 73 (D&I MacDonald); 79 (Mark Walker)
Frances M. Roberts: p. 56, 86

Cover photo: Hazel Hankin

The producer would like to thank Marcia Knoll for reviewing this manuscript.

Contents

Prologue — 5

1 **When Teens Drop Out** — 7
Problems for Individuals • Problems for the Nation • Who Drops Out? • Finding Reasons to Stay in School

2 **Special Learning Problems** — 17
What Are Learning Disabilities? • Specific Learning Disabilities • A Widespread Problem • Looking for Causes • Potential Problems • Identifying Learning Problems • Finding Help • Looking Toward the Future • College Programs for the Learning Disabled

3 **Dealing with Tough Situations** — 35
Coping with Family Problems • Homelessness • Violence in the Schools • Teen Pregnancy • Negative Influences • School Support Groups

4 **Making the Most of School** — 51
Falling Behind • Changing for the Better • Learning How to Learn • Organize for Success • A Time and Place to Study • Planning Study Sessions • Effective Notes • The Value of Reading • Mastering Writing Assignments • Taking Tests

5 **Alternatives to Dropping Out** — 71
Vocational Training • Returning to School • Helping Students Succeed • School Reforms • Helping Students at Risk • Community Involvement • Looking Toward the Future

Additional Resources — 90
For Further Reading — 92
Glossary — 94
Index — 95

Prologue

This book is about the choices young people make regarding their education—whether to stay in school or drop out, whether to make the most of the time they do spend in school or just get by, and how to prepare for the future.

For those of you who are seriously thinking of dropping out, it is hoped that this book will persuade you to change your mind or at least give the matter much more careful thought. If you are having trouble with school, there are ways to develop new skills or get help. If you are having personal or family problems, there are ways to cope without leaving school.

Sometimes there are tempting reasons to drop out. But young people who quit school before graduating often find themselves experiencing many more problems than they expected. Their choices in adult life can be severely limited because of a decision made during the teenage years. Dropping out also poses problems for society when people do not have the education or skills they need to support themselves and their families.

The United States likes to consider itself an economic and political leader, but it has a higher dropout rate than many other industrialized nations. This worried the nation's leaders so much that in 1989, the president met with all of the nation's governors at a special education summit meeting. That year, Congress adopted a set of national education goals. One of them is to decrease the nation's dropout rate to 10 percent or less by the year 2000. In the years since that meeting, many new programs have been proposed to improve our public education system. Our leaders know that in order to be strong, America needs well-educated citizens. People are a nation's most valuable resource.

Perhaps you have thought about dropping out yourself or have a friend who is considering this step. It is vital to think about it very carefully. Get the facts. Take your time. Find out all you can about what your choice will mean in your everyday life, both now and later on. Be sure you have tried your best and have used the resources that are available before you give up on school, or you may shortchange yourself and your future. By giving school another chance and making your best effort, you may find that you actually enjoy learning or can at least achieve your goal of graduating.

1
WHEN TEENS DROP OUT

*I've had it with school. It's a waste of time,
the things they want you to do.*
—Tommy, age 17

Each June, throughout America, proud families gather at high school graduation ceremonies. Wearing the traditional cap and gown, graduating seniors receive their diplomas and are congratulated on their achievement. They listen to speeches about the opportunities and challenges they now face as adults. "I worked hard for that diploma," a 19-year-old from Los Angeles recalls. "There were plenty of times I thought I wouldn't make it." Another graduate, from Seward Park High School in New York City, echoes that feeling. In her class, about 40 percent of those who began as freshmen did not finish high school.

Dropping out of high school is a serious problem in America. In the early 1990s, statistics from the U.S. Department of Education showed that about 30 percent (nearly one-third) of all U.S. students who had entered public high school as freshmen were dropping out before they graduated. Some areas have much higher dropout rates than others. In inner-city schools, rates can exceed 50 percent.

Large numbers of other students "drop out" mentally and fail to do their best in school. They may have little interest in learning during the years they spend in school. Some also need more help from their teachers, parents, and communities in order to

Nearly one-third of all high school students in the United States will never experience the joy of graduating.

succeed. These students may graduate without having gotten the most out of their years in school.

Around the nation, approximately a million teenagers drop out of school each year.

PROBLEMS FOR INDIVIDUALS

When young people leave school early or graduate poorly prepared for jobs and adult responsibilities, the human and economic costs can be high. One common problem is finding a job. Today's workplaces are competitive, with many people vying for the same jobs. Education Secretary Richard W. Riley has said, "Many dropouts say they left school because they were failing or just didn't like it. Some will come back and finish, but too many find themselves unemployed or stuck in a job with no future."

Before the mid-1900s, dropping out of school was not uncommon, but it posed far fewer problems for individuals and society. In early America, people often supported themselves through farming, small family-run businesses, or manual labor. Then, as the nation developed a manufacturing economy in the

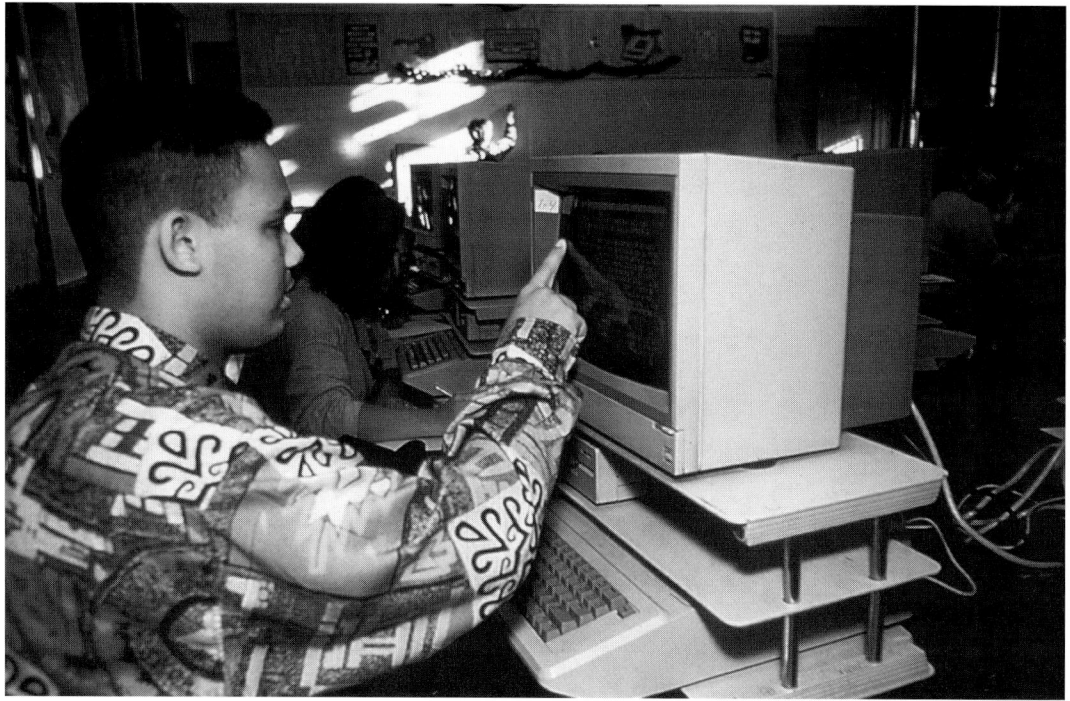

The jobs of today and the future require an educated work force. Workers without a high school diploma will be left out.

1800s and early 1900s, there were many jobs for unskilled or semiskilled workers. People with little or no education could find jobs in the steel, textile, or lumber industries. In factories, they could receive training to operate machines or work on assembly lines. A person who was out of work might live with his or her extended family, where members took care of one another and met their basic needs for food, shelter, and clothing.

Things are quite different today. Manufacturing jobs in the United States have steadily declined. Today, we need far more education than our ancestors did in order to find and keep a job in a complex, technological world. And most people hope for more than just any job. They want a good job, with decent wages and benefits such as health insurance, in order to support themselves and their children.

THE UNEDUCATED NEED NOT APPLY

Each year, American businesses spend about $25 billion on remedial training for workers who have not mastered basic skills in reading, writing, and mathematics. In an *ABC News Special* called "America's Kids: Teaching Them How to Think," business leaders discussed the importance of a good education. Lee Iacocca, the former chairman of Chrysler Corporation, said bluntly, "The factory of the future is highly technical, a lot of lasers, a lot of robotics, a lot of computers at every station. If [an employee] can't handle that kind of thing, he ain't gonna get a job, he's gonna get a broom."

Describing the needs of his company, Stan Stein, the vice-president of personnel at McDonald's, said, "We need people who can think on their feet, who can initiate, who can problem-solve, who can be team players." Although people might think that employees at fast-food restaurants have "easy" jobs, Stein and others disagree. They point out that employees must be able to handle hundreds of orders, use many different buttons on the cash registers, and communicate well with customers and co-workers.

Workers at textile plants may not require advanced college degrees, but they, too, need a solid education. Gene Gwaltney, the chairman of Russell Corporation, a manufacturer of sweatshirts and football jerseys, said, "A sense of reasoning and a sense of imagination is something that we really need here more than anything else." Russell's employees work in teams and must carefully plan what to do and how long their part of the project will take. They handle high-tech machinery instead of the thimble and thread devices that were once used. A Russell employee said, "They're going to start having more computers on a lot of the machines. Some have already got them. And people like me—couldn't run it."

Dropping out can dramatically affect a person's future. In a 1987 publication, the U.S. Department of Education said,

> *Leaving school can take a devastating human toll. A recent Gallup poll found that 23 percent of the respondents with less than a high school diploma were dissatisfied with their personal lives, compared with 14 percent of all respondents and only 6 percent of college graduates. Not surprisingly, many dropouts, even when surveyed shortly after leaving school, believed their decision to do so was a mistake. Dropouts even tend to have poorer health.*

Why poorer health? Statistics show that dropouts are more likely to be unemployed or employed in low-wage jobs. Such jobs may involve more physical labor and hazards in the workplace. Most part-time jobs do not include health insurance. Without enough money, a person usually cannot afford a high quality of food, shelter, and health care. Economic problems may also cause stress that can damage a person's health.

The U.S. Department of Commerce has determined that male dropouts earn about $441,000 less during their lifetimes than males who graduate from high school. Dropouts may find that they are automatically excluded from many jobs. For instance, a high school diploma is required to join the U.S. military.

PROBLEMS FOR THE NATION

The costs to society—in effect, to all citizens—are also high. Today, most people live in nuclear families rather than extended ones that include various relatives. Many live in different towns or cities than other family members. The unemployed tend to rely on government assistance for support, which increases the burdens on taxpayers.

High school dropouts make up the majority of people on welfare (public assistance). In addition, nearly three-fourths of the U.S. prison population consists of high school dropouts. The cost of keeping a person in prison is around $30,000 to $40,000 a year—more than it cost in 1995 to attend a top college such as Harvard University and far more than the cost of a year of high school.

In all, the cost of drug abuse, welfare, unemployment, and crime (all higher among dropouts) has been put at some $60 billion a year. There is also a great deal of competition in the world economic markets as different countries try to sell their goods and services. The nation's economic strength depends upon having a well-educated and well-trained work force. Yet America has a higher dropout rate than other industrialized nations, such as Japan, Canada, and Germany. American students often score lower on international achievement tests than students from other industrialized nations. David Kearns, the former chairman and chief economic officer of Xerox Corporation, expressed the concern of many business leaders when he said, "If we can't compete [in the world's economic markets], our nation as we know it today will not survive."

WHO DROPS OUT?

Studies have shown that there are many different reasons young people do not finish high school. When asked why they dropped out, people most often say that they hated or disliked school. "I was totally bored. I felt like school was a waste of time and getting me nowhere," says Simon, age 18, who dropped out after his junior year.

Fear of failing and school failure account for a high percentage of school dropouts. According to statistics, the best predictor of who will drop out before graduation is ongoing school failure. Students who earn good grades are far more likely to graduate than those who get Ds and Fs.

Students who have repeated one or more grades are also more likely to drop out. This was true of Linn A., who left school during her junior year. She says, "I was no good at school and everyone knows it. They made me repeat fifth grade. Even the teachers made me feel like a dummy." Another student, now 21,

Boredom, dislike of school, and poor grades are the biggest reasons for dropping out.

remembers, "One year, I missed a lot of school. I got behind in everything and didn't pass. There's no way I would go back to the same grade again, so I quit."

Language barriers can lead to early school failure that eventually leads a person to give up and drop out. Young people growing up in single-parent families where English is not the main language have higher dropout rates. Often, these are households headed by single women living in poverty.

Students with a history of being in trouble—tardiness, suspensions, problems with the law—also have higher dropout rates. Experts say that nonattendance in early grades is a big predictor of dropping out of school. Laurie Holmes, director of Education Network, an organization that works to reduce the dropout rate, said in 1990, "Kids who are going to drop out have twice as many absences by third grade."

Family and social problems account for large numbers of school dropouts. The number of unmarried teen mothers in every ethnic group has risen steadily since the 1970s. Many of these young women—80 percent in some school systems—drop out. A high number of them become dependent on welfare checks to support themselves and their children. Tonia R., a 17-year-old with a 7-month-old daughter, knows how hard it is to stay in school while caring for a baby. She says, "The only time I can study is when she's asleep. Usually I stay up most of the night." But Tonia is determined to stay in school. Her mother, who never married, had seven children by the time she was 24; she is an alcoholic who has never held a steady job. "I don't want to end up like her," says Tonia, who lives with her grandmother.

Tonia's grandmother cares about her schooling and encourages her to work hard. But many young people have no one at home to help them with homework, talk with their teachers, or even support the idea of working to get an education. Teachers at one New York City high school report that on Open School Nights, held early in the year, only about 12 percent of the parents come to meet teachers and hear about the courses. Some students bring their older brothers or sisters along to meet their teachers, but most have nobody to come with them.

Poverty creates obstacles to school success. Many young people succeed against the odds, but those living in poor urban or rural areas are at a higher risk of dropping out. Minorities, including African Americans, Hispanic Americans, and Native Americans, have higher dropout rates. Migrant workers and the homeless drop out much more often than middle-class students or those living in suburbs. This has been linked to poverty and related problems, since members of different ethnic groups have the same range of abilities as others. They can succeed when given the same opportunities.

Living in families and neighborhoods where there is violence, neglect, or substance abuse poses obstacles to school success. It is a struggle to stay in school while living in a home where one or more parents abuse alcohol or drugs or where you fear for your safety. One teacher in a Chicago inner-city school said, "Some of these kids struggle to survive. They live in housing projects where you fear for your life. They dodge drug dealers and gangs on their way to school. It's an accomplishment just to get here each day." In many neighborhoods, the pressure to use or sell drugs is intense. Schools are among the places where drugs are sold.

Besides that, schools located in poor neighborhoods may not have enough funds to maintain their buildings and pay for the programs they need. Much school funding comes from local taxes, and low-income areas raise less taxes than wealthier suburbs. Inner-city schools are often old and run-down, without the space, textbooks, equipment, or number of teachers and staff members found in suburban schools. There may be more students per class than in wealthier schools. Students attending large, overcrowded schools may feel that nobody cares about them or their education.

> **REASONS FOR DROPPING OUT**
>
> A 1994 report by the U.S. Department of Education listed the reasons students give for dropping out. The most common reason given was "hate or dislike school," cited by 43 percent of those who dropped out between tenth and twelfth grades. Others included:
>
> - chronically failing school or fear of failing
> - language barriers
> - teenage pregnancy
> - wanting to earn money now and to be on one's own
> - pressure from peers who do not stay in school
> - drug and alcohol problems that interfere with school
> - family problems

Some students leave school because they want to work full-time. "I felt like I could accomplish more getting a job and earning money," says Bill, age 20, who dropped out in his sophomore year. "We needed money at home, and I wanted to buy things other kids have and get a car." Statistics also show that students who work at jobs outside of school have higher dropout rates than those who work fewer hours or not at all. It takes extra effort and a strong commitment to handle a job and school at the same time.

Peer pressure can result in dropping out. "My boyfriend and some of the people we know quit school. It was more fun hanging out with them than going to school, any day. I kept getting behind until there was no way to catch up, so I quit," says Pam, age 16. Teens whose friends do not value school tend to share those attitudes.

Although personal and family problems and learning problems can lead some students to quit, many students drop out for more ordinary reasons. These may include a lack of motivation for learning or a lack of the skills needed to do

well in school. Disorganization and poor study skills can lead students to dislike school and get so far behind that dropping out seems like the solution. Studies show that most high school dropouts are as capable of learning as those who do not drop out.

There may be many reasons for dropping out, and they can be more complicated and multifaceted than they seem at first glance. Experts who have studied the problem see dropping out as a process, rather than a single event. It is a decision that evolves over a period of time, usually for more than one reason.

FINDING REASONS TO STAY IN SCHOOL

Whatever the reasons that teens have for giving up on school, efforts are being made throughout America to encourage teenagers to stay in school. There are programs to improve schools and provide young people with the support and services they need in order to succeed. Schools offer services such as counseling, tutoring, day care for students' children, and job training. Some are taking steps to reduce violence in the school and make their programs more personalized and meaningful for students. Such programs help many teens. They are described later in this book.

Some people have special learning disabilities that make school so difficult that they decide to quit. There are many resources available in and out of the schools to help students with these problems reach their potential. Chapter 2 describes learning disabilities and ways to deal with them.

At times, dropping out may seem like the best or even the only answer. But there are always choices, and there are resources for those who want to succeed in school. This book will discuss more about the dropout problem and tell what America as a whole is doing about it, along with ways that you can improve your own school experience.

Ultimately, many students realize that they are responsible for their own learning and their own futures. While it would be nice if school was always fun and interesting and the classes fit each individual's needs and wants, this is unlikely to happen in real life. But you can succeed in spite of difficulties. When a lack of motivation, effort, or skills is the problem, you can do a great deal to help yourself. You can learn to be a better student.

Bullying and violence in the schools is another common reason for dropping out. Students who don't feel safe in or near their school may stop attending.

2
SPECIAL LEARNING PROBLEMS

*I'd try to do the work, but I always took too long.
Finally, I just quit.*
—Rafael, age 16

Terri, age 15, doesn't hate the idea of learning. In fact, she is eager to learn and to do well in school. But school is a struggle. Even though she enjoys books, Terri finds that studying can be a frustrating process. She has trouble keeping track of what she reads as she goes along, and she has to look up the same words more than once in the dictionary in order to understand what she is reading. Writing assignments are another big problem. Terri can't seem to organize her ideas or find the right words to express her ideas. "My friends don't have this problem," says Terri. "It comes so easily for them."

Wes, a high school freshman, has had problems in school since first grade. His teachers are constantly telling him to sit still and pay attention. In fourth grade, he was held back a year because he failed two subjects. People call Wes a scatterbrain because he often forgets or misplaces things. He has also been told that he is bright but that he is "lazy" and "must try harder." But even when he tries, Wes has trouble concentrating on one task for very long. Reading long passages of social studies or science material seems impossible, yet Wes has a good memory and learns math easily. Overall, Wes finds school so discouraging that he has decided to quit as soon as he is old enough.

To succeed in school, students with learning disabilities need extra help—but often they don't get it. These students are at much greater risk of dropping out.

Jonathan, age 13, also struggles in school. He has had trouble keeping up with his classmates since third grade. It takes him longer to understand what the teacher is saying in class and to finish his lessons. He especially dreads being asked to read aloud. Jonathan has trouble with penmanship and other things that require physical coordination. When teams are picked for sports, he is often the last to be chosen. Lately, he has been worried that something is wrong with his brain. "Why am I so slow, so different?" he wonders, as he observes others who seem able to master things without effort.

Terri, Wes, and Jonathan are examples of students who have learning disabilities. Perhaps you or someone you know has experienced similar problems. Even though these teens have near-average to above-average intelligence, they find themselves struggling to get through school. Their learning disabilities—what some educators call "hidden handicaps"—keep them from reaching their potential.

Students who have undetected learning disabilities or who do not receive the help they need can become caught in a cycle of frustration and despair. Often, they choose to drop out rather than to keep struggling.

WHAT ARE LEARNING DISABILITIES?

People use the term "learning disability" to refer to gaps in the development of skills we need for learning—for instance, the ability to receive and understand information or to link information from different parts of the brain. These lags may affect our ability to read, write, compute, remember, coordinate physical movements, or understand oral or written instructions, among other things.

Of course, everyone has strengths and weaknesses, and some people may develop certain skills sooner or later than others do. Some children learn to ride a bicycle or to read earlier than other children of the same age. Some can draw intricate pictures but not understand number concepts as well as their peers. Most of us have some trouble learning a particular subject at some time during our school years. However, a serious lag in one or more basic skills can make learning quite difficult.

SPECIFIC LEARNING DISABILITIES

There are a number of different learning disabilities. Some people have problems with memory, either short-term memory (information that is remembered for a short time) or long-term memory (information that is stored for a long time or permanently). Eric H. has problems with auditory memory (the ability to remember what is heard) and in sequencing—the ability to do things in order or

Most students with learning disabilities have normal intelligence, but they may need extra time to complete their assignments.

in logical steps. This makes it hard for him to recall and follow a series of directions. Until he was 11, adults often criticized and punished Eric for disobedience. He felt relieved when a teacher realized he had a learning disability and his school began helping him find ways to deal with it.

Keisha M. has another kind of learning problem, a deficit in the area of visual processing (the ability to perceive information that comes in through the eyes, or visual sense). It is hard for Keisha to copy what she sees written on the chalkboard or printed in her textbooks. As a result, her reading and writing skills have suffered. When she was still having problems reading simple sentences in the third grade, her teacher recommended that she be tested for learning disabilities. After the school understood the problem, they began helping Keisha to cope with her "learning difference." It takes her more time to finish some assignments, but Keisha can do them when she is given that time.

One of the best-known learning disabilities is dyslexia, sometimes called specific language difficulty. This disturbance in the ability to deal with words can cause serious problems in learning to read, speak, or write. People with dyslexia may have trouble sorting out and decoding, or interpreting, the symbols that make up words. They may reverse letters or use them in the wrong sequence. Spelling and handwriting are often difficult. Specialized teaching based on the students' specific needs can help them learn these skills.

Some well-known people, including actor Tom Cruise, Olympic gold medalist Bruce Jenner, and singer-actress Cher, have described their experiences with dyslexia. Former First Lady Barbara Bush, a literacy advocate, has said that one of her sons received special help for this problem during his school years.

About 20 percent of children with learning disabilities have attention problems. People with attention deficit disorder (ADD) are easily distracted and have trouble paying attention and sitting still. They are often impulsive and may speak, act, or lose their tempers before thinking about the consequences. Many cannot focus on one activity for very long and tend to daydream. Some people have attention deficit disorder with hyperactivity, or ADHD. This condition is characterized by excess energy and physical activity and a need for high levels of stimulation. A child with ADHD may be described as "climbing the walls."

Edward M. Hallowell, a psychiatrist and expert on ADD, realized during a medical school lecture on ADD that he, himself, had this condition. In his book *Driven to Distraction,* Hallowell writes that during his school years, he was often called "a daydreamer," "lazy," "an underachiever," "a spaceshot." He felt relieved when he discovered there was a reason for

> . . . the conversations I tuned out of, involuntarily, for no apparent reason. For the rage I felt and the times I broke pencils and threw them around the room when I didn't immediately grasp a concept in grade school. For the seven attempts it can take me to read a page of a novel.

For . . . forgetting the task at hand as I go off on the wings of a new thought or off in search of what I forgot . . .

There are many other types of learning problems, and different people may have various combinations of one or more of them. Everyone is unique and must look for solutions that work best for their particular combination of strengths and weaknesses.

A WIDESPREAD PROBLEM

It is estimated that between 4 and 5 million school-age children in America have learning disabilities. Most experts agree that at least 10 percent of all children are educationally handicapped in some way. The number may be as high as 25 percent—one in every four children—or even higher. While some learning problems are mild, from 3 to 7 percent of these children have problems severe enough to require special schooling. Some of these students attend special education programs in public schools or private schools that specialize in particular learning disabilities. The majority of people with learning disabilities are placed in regular classrooms and receive extra help from their teachers and others within the school system.

A large proportion of those with learning disabilities are male, although nobody knows for certain why this is true. Statistics show that for every girl with learning disabilities, there are about seven boys. Lately, some experts have questioned these statistics. They are wondering whether teachers notice boys' problems earlier and more often because their behavior tends to be more active and aggressive than that of girls.

Overall, the number of people with learning disabilities has risen since the 1950s. This may be because today's educators are more aware of learning problems than they were in the past. Since the 1960s, a greater effort has been made to diagnose and treat learning disorders. Before that time, some children with these problems were mistakenly labeled as having psychological problems or even mental retardation. They got through school as best they could, often feeling miserable, or they dropped out.

LOOKING FOR CAUSES

Researchers aren't sure what causes all types of learning disabilities. Some can result from a head injury, illness, exposure to toxic substances (such as drugs, alcohol, or lead), or a serious problem during pregnancy or childbirth. Heredity seems to play an important role, since certain learning problems run in families.

Some researchers claim there is a connection between learning disabilities and allergies or sensitivities to certain foods, food dyes, and preservatives, or to chemicals in the environment.

In a publication called "Learning Disabilities," the National Institute of Mental Health says, "New evidence seems to show that most learning disabilities do not stem from a single, specific area of the brain, but from difficulties in bringing together information from various brain regions."

In many cases, no specific cause for learning disabilities can be identified. Research into the brain and nervous system may eventually tell us why they occur. Whatever the cause, people can learn to compensate for their disabilities. They can develop other ways to learn and use their strengths to succeed.

POTENTIAL PROBLEMS

Learning problems can lead to low self-esteem and other difficulties. At a support group meeting for students with learning disabilities, several teens described having felt guilt, anger, frustration, and a sense of incompetence. "I feel so out of it sometimes," said Jakama, age 16. "It would be so nice just to be the smart one sometimes, instead of the one people think is dumb." "Why do I have to be different?" 14-year-old Tiffany often asks her mother. "Why does it have to be so hard for me?" It's hard feeling different from others, especially during the teen years.

Many teens hesitate to try after experiencing years of failure. Their sense of defeat grows as they watch classmates progress with less trouble. They may give up and believe they are unable to reach their goals in life.

Author Sally L. Smith, the mother of a grown son with learning disabilities, is the founder of a special school for such students in Washington, D.C. She writes that an adolescent with learning disabilities often has the feeling that "everybody's picking on me.... Often he sees his world as a series of mistakes, one after another, all totaling personal disaster. It's hard to grow up feeling good about himself under these conditions." Smith says that many students with learning disabilities may even fear that they have some sort of brain disease or mental retardation. She writes, "He's angry at the world's demands on him, demands he cannot meet. He's angry at himself for not being able to do what he wants to do. He's angry at his parents, teachers, brothers, sisters, neighbors, and classmates for seeing him in the act of not being able to."

Students who seem to daydream in class or have trouble paying attention may actually have a learning disability called attention deficit disorder.

Young people may react to the situation by developing behavior problems. Some become shy and withdrawn, while others show hostility and engage in antisocial behavior. They may become the "class clown" or act disruptive in other ways.

In his book *Dyslexia*, author John F. Savage describes the problems and vicious cycle that can come from dyslexia:

> *Children with dyslexia usually get off to a bad start in school. First graders spend most of their time learning to read and write, and this emphasis continues for the next two grades as well. Because reading and writing are major problem areas, dyslexic children experience failure and frustration very early in their school years. They become known as "hard to teach." Teachers tell them to "pay attention." Parents tell them to "try harder." What seems to work well for most children doesn't seem to work for them at all.*

It is not surprising that many students, faced with this kind of frustration, drop out of school. A high number of high school dropouts, estimated to be from 45 to 75 percent, have learning disabilities. Students with learning disabilities may have to repeat grades. Those who have repeated one or more grades are

twice as likely to drop out, according to a 1994 study. Those who have never been held back have a dropout rate of 9.4 percent; those who have been held back have a rate of 19.8 percent. Of those students who have been held back more than one time, the dropout rate rises to 40.9 percent.

Researchers also say that at least 75 percent of all delinquent teens have learning disabilities. Another survey shows that three out of four children who are sent for psychological services have some type of learning disability. Likewise, a high percentage of the people in America's prisons are high school dropouts with learning disabilities. Without help, teens with serious learning disabilities are at high risk for many problems later on.

Many who leave school find themselves unemployed or in jobs that do not interest them. Some go from job to job as they experience the same kinds of personal and learning problems that kept them from doing well in school.

A great deal can be done to prevent and alleviate these problems. With hard work and support from teachers, family, and others, people with learning disabilities can learn and develop their talents.

IDENTIFYING LEARNING PROBLEMS

Some learning problems are noticed when children are quite young. Matthew C. began receiving special help while he was still in pre-school. A perceptive teacher saw that he had a great deal of trouble following directions and paying attention. At age four, he did not speak in full sentences. For two years, Matthew attended a special education pre-school where three carefully trained teachers worked with eight students. In first grade, he attended a regular classroom and went to speech and language therapy sessions three times a week. Now in second grade, Matthew still receives speech and language therapy and has his reading classes in a small, quiet resource room at school, where a teacher works with small groups of students to be sure they understand each lesson and master basic skills, step by step.

Lizelle P. has received special help since first grade. Now in ninth grade, she attends some regular, or "mainstream," classes and some special education classes. When she needs more help, her teachers work with her before or after school. Lizelle plans to finish school, which will make her the first in her family to graduate. Her two older brothers both dropped out. "I think they may have the same problems in school like I do, but nobody said that to my parents," says Lizelle. "They didn't like school and they gave up on it."

By some estimates, 75 percent or more of all delinquent teens suffer from learning disabilities. Ironically, it is often only when these young people are in detention that their problem is diagnosed.

Dealing with learning problems early is ideal, but some young people go from grade to grade, struggling to learn, and not understanding why they are having so much trouble. Adam F. has dyslexia, but his problem was not recognized until he reached the eighth grade. Quiet and helpful, Adam did not cause any trouble in the classroom. On his own, he managed to scrape by, although school was an ongoing struggle. His teachers tended to give Adam "the benefit of the doubt," even though he was not learning what he should, because of his pleasant personality. Adam says, "I wish I didn't have to be different. I didn't like having to leave class to go to a special room for help. But it's better than before, when I didn't know what was wrong. It's really better to find out I can read and do the work if I learn the right way."

How can you tell if someone has a learning disability that is causing problems in school? That decision is usually made by a team of education specialists—teachers, school psychologists, and speech and language pathologists, for example. A medical doctor, such as a pediatrician or neurologist (doctor who deals with problems in the central nervous system) may also become involved. Since there is no conclusive physical test to "show" learning disabilities, specialists ask people about their background and problems in school.

A school psychologist or other specialist may use various tests to find out a student's strengths and weaknesses. The tests may compare his or

SIGNS OF LEARNING DISABILITY

These traits may be signs of learning disabilities:

- Problems in early life, such as being slow to crawl, walk, speak
- Persistent difficulty in learning despite intelligence that is at least normal
- Being easily distracted or unable to concentrate
- Hyperactivity
- Inconsistency
- Awkwardness; poor balance; clumsy physical movements
- Trouble with skills that require fine-motor coordination, such as drawing and handwriting
- Difficulty following directions
- Left-right confusion
- Impulsive behavior and inability to wait
- Poor speech and language skills
- Trouble beginning, planning, and completing a task
- Trouble reading—cannot recall the sounds each letter makes; problems recalling words known before
- Feeling confused while listening to directions
- Fidgety, overactive behavior
- Difficulty judging size, distance, direction
- Trouble recognizing difference between some letters, such as b and d
- A "scattering of achievement": may be very good at math, for example, but have trouble with reading or writing

Learning-disabled students in this special program in Missouri work at their own pace in a special classroom. The program has cut the local drop-out rate in half.

her skills with those considered to be normal for a person of that age and intelligence. For example, some tests measure a person's reading level or the ability to understand language. These tests may show what areas of learning are a problem—for example, weaknesses in the area of auditory memory (remembering what is heard); visual discrimination (seeing the differences among various shapes, numbers, and letters); understanding abstract ideas; recalling things learned in the past. This information is used by teachers to plan ways to help the student learn best in his or her own way.

FINDING HELP

If you suspect you or someone you care about might have a learning disability and would like help, talk with your parents, teachers, and school guidance counselor or psychologist. Request an evaluation and meetings with school staff members to discuss what can be done.

Federal laws state that students with learning disabilities are entitled to certain services. The Individuals with Disabilities Education Acts of 1990 and 1991 guarantee an appropriate public education from age 5 to 19 to any person diagnosed with a learning disability. The act requires schools to design and implement an Individualized Education Program (IEP) that will meet the student's needs.

States have different procedures and guidelines that determine who is eligible to receive special services. School systems differ in the ways in which they evaluate students and provide services, and services differ from school to school. Individuals and families can get help in locating resources they need through their state department of education and local support groups for people with learning disabilities. The National Center for Children and Youth can put you in touch with local resources and state agencies that can help. Advocacy agencies and client assistance programs offer legal assistance when schools fail to respond to a student's needs.

For those who have already dropped out of school, help is still out there. The state department of education can refer you to an agency that evaluates people and recommends programs to further their education or train them for certain job opportunities. Local adult education programs and the state department of vocational rehabilitation can also provide help and information. Even people who dropped out of school years ago can find help through literacy programs, adult education, and state agencies. A number of resources and support groups are listed at the end of this book.

PUBLIC LAW 94-142

THE EDUCATION OF ALL HANDICAPPED CHILDREN ACT

Passed by Congress in 1975, Public Law 94-142 protects the rights of students with learning disabilities. The law states that all children have the right to a free and appropriate public education. People aged 3 to 22 who are defined as handicapped are entitled to special instruction that meets their needs. They have the right to an evaluation that determines their educational needs and to a plan for a program that will meet those goals.

The law also defines the rights of parents whose children are defined as handicapped. They have the right to information about their child's education and can take part in the planning process as major educational decisions are being made for their child.

Under the law, disabled children are to be educated with their non-disabled peers to the fullest extent possible. Children are to be in the "least restrictive environment" that can meet their educational needs.

Every learning-disabled student is entitled to an appropriate education. Working with a tutor is often part of a student's individualized education program.

If the school determines that someone has learning disabilities and qualifies for help, the school will arrange an educational planning meeting. At this meeting, the education team discuss an individual's educational goals and how to achieve them. Strengths and weaknesses are clearly defined, and the group discusses the best teaching methods, teachers, and classroom placements.

Services are usually provided through the special education department at the school. It provides more individualized teaching for children who do not learn by the same methods that work for most other students. Children who are very gifted also receive special education services so that they can work in a more individualized way. Special ed classes are usually smaller and tailored to the students' particular needs. Since they have fewer students, teachers can give each one more help, while students move at their own pace.

Students may spend the whole day or just part of the day in special classes. When learning in a regular classroom has been frustrating and negative, this change can turn learning into a pleasant and rewarding experience. The purpose of a school is, after all, to help people learn and that includes people who learn in different ways.

LOOKING TOWARD THE FUTURE

According to expert Sally L. Smith, "The learning-disabled person needs a realistic view of his strengths and capabilities as well as his weaknesses and disabilities, to make the most of what he has. Nothing is more pathetic than the person who pretends to be what he is not, who chases after impossible goals, destroying himself along the way. This is not to say that the learning-disabled adolescent should settle for the lowest practical opportunities, without aiming higher. For many, a college education is possible and attainable. Junior colleges and community colleges are becoming a haven for young learning-disabled adults after they leave high school. The time they gain there often gives them the opportunity to mature, to find a specialty, to develop organization, discipline, and study habits that will enable them to succeed."

What happens after high school? People with learning disabilities can look forward to many things—further education, satisfying careers, happy personal lives. Colleges and universities that receive public funding are required to develop programs that make it easier for students with learning disabilities to attend. Many recruit students with disabilities and provide the services they need to succeed in college. Your library may have a book that can help you. It is called *Peterson's Guide to Colleges with Programs for Learning Disabled Students,* edited by Charles T. Mangrum II and Stephen S. Strichert. Other books and organizations listed at the back of this book can also help you choose a program that will be right for you.

SUCCESS STORIES

When asked to name the most famous scientist of the twentieth century, many of us immediately think of Albert Einstein. A brilliant physicist, Einstein developed many important scientific ideas. Yet during Einstein's school years, his teachers considered him to be a slow learner. His language skills were behind those of his peers. Later, he had to take the admission test twice before he passed and was admitted to the university. Education experts now are convinced that Albert Einstein had learning disabilites.

A number of other well-known people overcame learning disabilities. Thomas Edison, inventor of the light bulb and phonograph among other things, was also a school failure. His teachers complained that he was noisy, overly active, disobedient, and would never amount to much. In despair, Edison's mother removed him from school and taught him at home, helping him to become a brilliant inventor. It is said that Edison had tried making a thousand light bulbs before he made one that worked. When he was asked how it felt to fail a thousand times, Edison said, "I didn't fail a thousand times. The light bulb was an invention with a thousand steps."

Some people find that their disabilities have turned out to be an asset. "It taught me to work hard," says Rachel, a 24-year-old college graduate who maintained a B+ average while earning her degree. "I learned to try harder than some of the kids who were always able to pass without much effort. At my job now, my boss frequently tells me I am one of the best organized and most productive members of our team." Like some students, Rachel took a year off between high school and college to work, travel, and prepare herself mentally for the challenge of college.

A 35-year-old business executive who struggled with learning disabilities in school says, "My parents always told me it was important to do certain things well in any job: be on time, be reliable, be pleasant, watch other people who are good at their jobs and learn from them. Doing these things has helped me in every job I had."

COLLEGE PROGRAMS FOR THE LEARNING DISABLED

Chris L., a college student, was embarrassed but determined. A student at a community college in New Jersey, she approached her psychology professor after class and told him that she had a learning disability. She needed to take tests in a quiet office, away from the distractions of the group. Chris has problems both with processing written material and with numbers.

At one time, students with learning disabilities might have been discouraged from attending college. Or they might have assumed they could never make it through a college program. Today, dozens of colleges and universities offer help, sometimes free, to students with disabilities. There are learning specialists, counselors, student-led support groups, learning resource centers, and tutors. Students can work out special arrangements with teachers, such as taking tests in a quiet place, as Chris L. does. They may ask for help in the form of tape-recorded notes or a note-taker who attends class with them.

At some colleges, students can take classes especially designed for people with learning disabilities. At others, they attend the same classes as other students, perhaps with adjustments.

Statistics from the American Council on Education, gathered in 1991, show that about 2.2 percent of the nation's college freshmen (about 1.6 million that year) identify themselves as having at least one learning disability. These figures have been steadily rising and are continuing to rise.

Some students choose not to tell anyone about their disabilities and to handle any problems that arise on their own. At certain colleges, where there are no special programs, this may be the smoothest path.

When preparing to apply to college, students who can verify that they have learning disabilities may ask to take the Scholastic Aptitude Test (SAT) sep-

Many junior and community colleges now offer special programs for learning-disabled students.

arately, in a quiet place, or be allowed additional time. In 1993, 27,000 students asked for this kind of accommodation. More college students than ever before asked for special consideration in taking tests for admission to graduate school, medical school, and law school. Some colleges also are willing to give less weight to test scores and grades when students have learning disabilities, since these may not reflect their actual ability.

For many students, being able to attend college is a great victory. Says Dawn, a junior at a university in Connecticut, "I was one of the slowest readers in elementary school. Teachers always told me I wasn't trying hard enough. When I found out about my disability in fifth grade, it was a relief. Still, I never got good grades in high school. I almost gave up the idea of ever going to college." Still, Dawn persisted. She attended a month-long summer program at a local college that taught study skills, test preparation, and other skills needed in college. With the help of recorded notes and some tutoring, Dawn is getting Cs and Bs. She says she is "thrilled" to be receiving a college education.

APPLYING TO COLLEGE

If students wish to discuss their learning disability when applying to college, experts make these suggestions:

- Have an up-to-date evaluation done during high school. This is available free of charge under the Disabilities Education Act.

- Be able to describe accurately the specific difficulties you have and the tasks that pose problems.

- Take an active part in discussions about your educational planning and future. Prepare to be your own advocate once you are at college.

- Find out about services at the colleges you might wish to attend—counseling, tutoring, support groups, and the like.

- Meet the staff at the office that works with students who have learning disabilities, if possible.

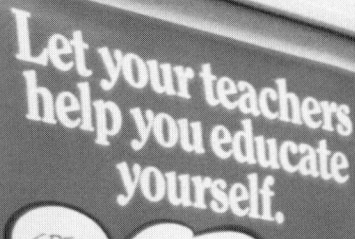

3
DEALING WITH TOUGH SITUATIONS

There were fights all the time at my high school. The building was in such bad shape you couldn't use the bathrooms. The teachers didn't care and neither did I. I just wanted to get out.
—Maya, age 15

Some problems go beyond weak study skills or the need for extra help with reading. Teenagers may face personal crises or ongoing problems at home or at school that are far more complex. These problems can become so overwhelming that there is no way to focus on schoolwork.

This happened to Derek, age 16. He found himself feeling depressed and nervous most of the time. When he got home from school, he did not feel like doing anything, including studying or being with friends. He would go to his room, close the door, and lie down in the dark, doing nothing or listening to the same music over and over.

As time went on, Derek felt more and more worthless and decided that he wanted to die. He found himself thinking of different ways to end his life. Meanwhile, Derek's grandmother, with whom he lived, had become more and more concerned. She took him to a community mental health center where he started attending counseling sessions and received medication for depression from a physician.

If you are feeling depressed or suicidal like Derek, or overwhelmed by other emotions, you may need to find help and find it fast. Maybe you can confide in someone you trust. There is help available,

Many girls drop out of high school because they are pregnant. Today many school systems have special programs to help pregnant girls stay in school and graduate.

and someone can steer you to the right place. Your local telephone book will have a list of hot-line numbers you can use if you feel you cannot confide in someone you know. If you are facing an emergency, you may need to dial 911 for immediate medical help.

For ongoing problems, you might find a good support group or counseling through your school, family physician, religious organization, or a community mental health center. There are other community programs available to help young people handle different kinds of problems. You are not alone.

COPING WITH FAMILY PROBLEMS

Besides their own emotional or health problems, many teens find themselves struggling with family problems. Some of them are relatively common—your older sister is too bossy or you and your parents disagree about how late you should stay out at night, what you should wear, whom you should socialize with, or your future plans. Although these kinds of disagreements may be annoying, they can sometimes be resolved if the people involved take time to listen, understand each other's point of view, and work out a plan that everyone can live with.

Other family problems are more serious—domestic violence, alcohol or drug abuse, sexual abuse, extreme poverty, parents who neglect their children. Unfortunately, such problems seem to be on the rise. A 1994 report issued by the Carnegie Corporation shows that since the 1970s, the United States has seen an increase in child abuse, premature births, and a decline in children's readiness for school. All of these can affect the physical and mental health of young people and hinder their school performance. Statistics show that it is harder for children living in poor, single-parent homes to do well in school. In addition, an estimated 70 percent of juvenile offenders come from single-parent homes where they have faced poverty and other difficulties.

Between 1985 and 1991, the number of child abuse victims rose by about 40 percent. Approximately one-third of these victims are babies less than one year old. Psychologists point out the rage that can develop in a person who is abused as a child. Cathy Spatz Widom, a professor of criminal justice at State University of New York at Albany, points out that abused children may decide that nobody cares about them and develop the attitude, "Why should I care about anyone else?"

Many families live in poverty, defined by the federal government as annual income below $14,764 for a family of four. By 1995, one in every four children in America was living in poverty. Among certain minority groups and in some rural and inner-city areas, this rate is even higher, nearly one in every two children.

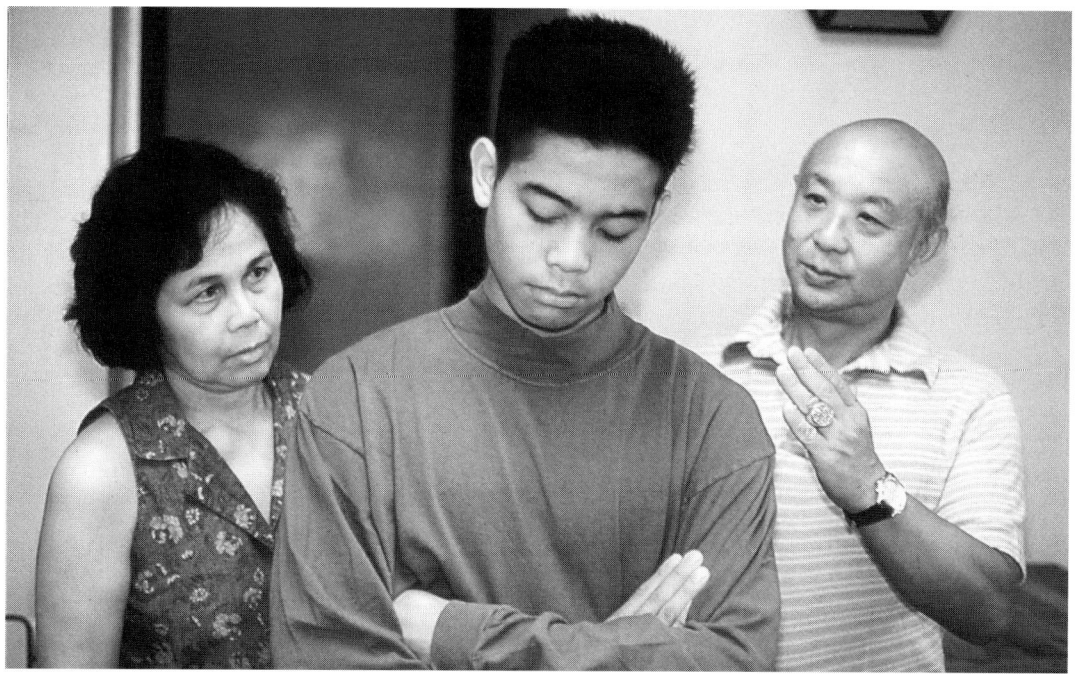

Family pressures are another reason for dropping out. Students who are having difficulties with their parents may have trouble concentrating on their schoolwork.

The number of single parents trying to raise children alone has risen steadily since the 1960s. By 1994, about half of all American children were living with only one parent. In two-parent families, both parents often work to make ends meet. During the time they are at home, they may be tired and busy. It is also less common today for people to live in extended families, sharing a home with grandparents and other relatives.

As a result, more young people find themselves with less adult help and supervision than in past generations. At the end of the school day, millions of young people go to a home where no adults are present. There are limited after-school programs for teenagers, and some families cannot find affordable day care for younger children.

During his childhood, Manny, a New Yorker now in his twenties, endured poverty, violence from his stepfather, and neglect from his mother. He claims that he had to raise himself on the streets, where he saw more violence. Manny says, "I guess I've known violence all my life, since I was about five or six when my stepfather started brutalizing me."

Deena, age 14, has been dealing with her parents' problems for a long time. Two years ago, her father was convicted of selling drugs and was sentenced to prison. Her mother, an alcoholic, has also been in trouble with the law. The court determined that Deena's mother could not take proper care of her, so she has been in and out of several foster homes. This has meant changing schools five times in the past few years, with different teachers and courses and many other adjustments. So that she could finish her most recent year of school at the same place, Deena went to live in a group home for teenage girls. She envies her friends who have more stable lives and loving families.

How does Deena cope? A thoughtful, caring person, she has some good friends who are very loyal to her. She has taken advantage of school services and makes an appointment to see a guidance counselor whenever she needs to talk. She does her best in school and joins other activities, such as sports, where she can meet people and gain self-confidence. "I try to remind myself that my parents' problems are their problems and it doesn't mean I'm a bad person," she says. "If I mess up in school or get into trouble, I could end up like them, and I don't want that."

Naomi, who just graduated from a California high school and is saving money for college, found that school helped her to handle a traumatic homelife with her mother and stepfather. School was something that she could count on every day; it gave her life a focus. She says, "I would not be here if it was not for school. I had a few really good people in my life that were on the faculty and had known about me ever since I started school. I didn't have to say a word to them, they just knew and they were there for me time and again." Doing her homework helped Naomi to feel more capable and gave her the sense that she was making progress in her life. She also attended support groups run by the school.

HOMELESSNESS

Nobody is certain how many American children are homeless, but estimates range from 500,000 to 750,000. About a third of the people in homeless shelters are families. Such children often miss school and face many barriers to school achievement. Without a home, students may not have regular meals, clean clothing, or even a place to keep their belongings. They may be living in a car or share space in crowded, noisy shelters. Often, they are surrounded by crime and drugs. Studying is nearly impossible.

The principal of a California school that serves many homeless children says that they often have "great gaps in learning." As a group, homeless children score lower on achievement tests and in their courses. Fewer than 50 percent were reading at their grade level, and they were more likely to be held back a grade, increasing their risk of dropping out. Yet they certainly have the same range of abilities as other young people.

When a family is on the move or going from one shelter to another, the children may be at one school for only a few weeks before moving to a different one. To ease part of this problem, Boston and some other cities allow students to

Homeless students often have to change schools several times in an academic year. This can so disrupt their progress that they drop out. In an effort to help these students keep up, some homeless shelters offer classes for residents.

stay at the same school even if they move to a different homeless shelter. New York City has tried a program in which teachers hold classes at shelters. Other cities have developed special schools solely for homeless children near shelters where they live.

A federal law called the Stewart McKinney Homeless Assistance Act of 1987 requires schools to provide an education to homeless children, along with other services to meet their extra needs. Schools may have difficulty finding the funding they need, which comes from local and federal government sources. Still, educators often make extra efforts to help students. One New York City principal, Terrence Quinn, says that coming to school is even more important for homeless children. Often, he says, it is the only place in the child's life that "offers warmth, stability, and hope." In his school, young people have been given school supplies they need, as well as items like alarm clocks to help them get up on time. Quinn advocates providing counseling, health care, tutoring, meals, and transportation services for homeless students. He also thinks they should be able to do their homework in the school, since this may be the only place they can study.

Like a number of other social problems, homelessness is a problem that our society still needs to deal with. Many people are appalled that in a nation as rich as America, people are living on the streets and some children have no homes. Numerous organizations work to help homeless people find jobs, housing, food, and health care, but not everyone is getting all the help they need.

VIOLENCE IN THE SCHOOLS

In March 1995, local news reporters in New York City carried a disturbing story. Young people at some of the city's schools had been beaten up at school by bullies. The reason? The victims had made the honor roll, and their assailants wanted to "punish them" for doing well. A fourth-grader told a reporter that he had been attacked and hit or beaten more than once that school year for the same reason. "They get mad if you get good grades," he said.

The problem of school violence, ranging from assaults to rapes to murders, has alarmed many Americans. Statistics about school violence show that each month about 300,000 students are physically attacked at secondary schools. More than 100,000 teachers are assaulted each year by students. On any given day, 6,250 teachers are threatened with assault. Educators point out that teachers cannot teach well and students cannot learn when they are worried about their physical safety in or around school.

Violent incidents range from being hit or pushed to being raped, stabbed, or shot. A number of violent incidents are related to drug and gang activities. In Washington, D.C., Chicago, New York, Atlanta, Miami, and Los Angeles, among other cities, teens have been shot and killed while walking to or from school. Teachers and principals have been killed. Staff members have been attacked or robbed in school parking lots. Students have been killed or hurt because they "dissed" another student—spoke or behaved in a way that others felt were disrespectful—or because they wore colors linked to a local gang. Students attending schools in areas plagued by violence express fear that they will be attacked. They say that another student might hurt them or even shoot them in order to take money, jewelry, or sneakers and other items of clothing.

Some students bring guns or other weapons to school. According to the National School Safety Center, more than 135,000 students take a gun to school each year. In past years, students who got into fights might use their fists or a knife, but today they often use guns. Guns can be bought on the street, sometimes for as little as $25, but many students bring them from home. There are more than 211 million privately owned guns in America. In some states, including Texas and Florida, about 60 percent of all households have one or more guns.

The presence of guns is not limited to high schools. About 13 percent of all incidents involving guns in school occurred in pre-school and elementary schools, according to 1993 statistics from the Federal Bureau of Investigation, Juvenile Justice Department.

Joe Clark is a principal who became well-known for instilling discipline and higher standards at his Paterson, New Jersey, high school during the 1980s. He described the dire problems facing many schools in poor cities: "These schools are constant bedlam. There are fights every day. There is widespread incompetence, wanton destruction of property, and constant vile language. . . . Prostitution is rampant. Violence is extolled. Weapons are prized and used. Drugs are king. The main role-model for inner-city youth is the rich drug dealer. The main point of distribution is the school."

Reggie, a teenager from Indianapolis, agrees, saying that anyone who walks to his school will see kids fighting and getting stabbed and hear the sound of gunfire nearby. According to Reggie, "The cops don't even drive by the schools anymore. It's not even worth their time. There's violence everywhere all the time. And if you don't see it yourself, flip on the TV and you'll see it in the news." Believing they are surrounded by danger, teens who don't even like guns may start to carry them anyway, to protect themselves.

Violence in the schools has become an increasingly serious problem. Every school day thousands of students and teachers are threatened or assaulted.

In some violence-plagued schools, students are searched with metal detectors to find guns, knives, and other weapons.

Gangs are an additional problem for high school students. Gang members pressure teenagers to join. Many do, either to feel part of the group or out of simple self-protection. Once in the gang, members find that gang activities—which often include drug dealing and fighting with other gangs—leave them little time for school. Teens who get involved in gangs usually drop out.

To deal with violence and gangs, schools have developed security procedures and programs aimed at prevention. In some cases, there are armed guards on school premises and metal detectors at the doors. Dogs are used to sniff out drugs. The building doors are locked after students and staff members are safely inside. A teacher who works in a New York City school that has both guards and metal detectors says, "It is depressing that we have come to this. The actions of a few have meant that the good kids, the ones who stay out of trouble, must attend school in this kind of atmosphere. But what are you going to do? The choice is to have the metal detectors and other security in place and maintain some safety at school or to risk a tragedy."

Some schools have gun-safety classes and education programs. Those caught bringing guns into school may be required to get counseling. In Boston, such students are sent to a local counseling center for five to ten days. While there, they receive counseling and educational evaluations. As part of the program, they visit local jails and meet violent offenders. Before leaving the program, they must develop a plan for improving their behavior and dealing with problems at home or school. Other similar programs have been developed at schools in Florida, California, and Michigan.

Some schools have set up groups or classes where students learn nonviolent ways to handle conflict. They learn better communication skills and ways to deal with peer pressure through assertiveness. They also learn how to disagree or state their opinions without using insults or other statements that may trigger violence. James Garbarino, of the Family Life Development Center at Cornell University, has written a workbook called "Let's Talk About Living in a World with Violence." The book is often used in school programs that help young people talk about their feelings and find nonviolent ways to express anger.

Other schools use student mediation to handle conflicts nonviolently. Hundreds of American schools use these programs, in which a council or third party mediates—helps to settle—disputes among others. At a conflict-mediation program in one Toledo high school, forty-four incidents were successfully resolved during the first seven months of the 1994–1995 school year. At the Teens on Target program in Oakland, California, some students receive special training in conflict resolution. They make themselves available to help others in the schoolyards where fights tend to break out.

Communities have set up street patrols or volunteer groups of adults who make sure young people can get to and from school safely. Teens have organized their own safety groups for getting to and from school.

The problem of violence in society is one that frustrates many Americans, including government leaders and law enforcement officials. In 1994, young people were among those who testified at special congressional hearings on crime and violence. They told lawmakers about violence in their neighborhoods and expressed hopes that something could be done to improve things.

TEEN PREGNANCY

When Jenelle became pregnant at age 15, she intended to stay in school. She gave birth to her son and continued to go to class while her grandmother helped her care for the baby. But life became difficult. She was often tired and fell behind in every subject. It was frequently too much trouble to get to class. Caring for the baby and working part-time at a grocery store left her with little time or energy to study. By the middle of her junior year, Jenelle had dropped out.

There are more than 500,000 teenage mothers nationwide. One of the major reasons teenage girls drop out of school is pregnancy and motherhood. Between 75 and 80 percent of all teenage mothers dropped out of school. A 1994 study by the U.S. Department of Education showed that about 25 percent of all the girls who drop out of school said it was due to pregnancy. Becoming fathers accounted for about 8 percent of male dropouts.

The costs of teenage pregnancy run high when mothers do not finish school and lack enough money to support themselves and their children. The federal government spends about $30 billion a year providing social services to teenagers and their babies. Only about 5 percent of teenage mothers receive college degrees compared to 47 percent of women who have their first child at age 25 or older. About one-third of the daughters born to teenage mothers will themselves have babies when they are teens.

Many schools have programs designed to prevent teen pregnancy and to help teen mothers stay in school. Schools sponsor health education programs that encourage self-control and abstinence from sexual activity. They educate students about birth control to prevent pregnancy. In some places, students can get birth control devices at school clinics.

Programs to help teen mothers stay in school frequently offer child care and parenting classes. One widely praised program is GRADS—Graduation, Reality, and Dual-role Skills—which began in Ohio. Among the services offered in GRADS are day care, counseling, and support groups. By 1985, the dropout rate for teens enrolled in GRADS was about 16 percent, much lower than the nationwide average.

After studying programs in Ohio and other states, child development and family sociology specialist Janet Barnett founded a successful program at the Norwich Free Academy in Connecticut. Barnett said, "I became very concerned because so many of the students who were dropping out of school were pregnant or young mothers. There would be more and more absences until, gradually, the student dropped out." In the Norwich program, mothers study child development, stress management, nutrition, and other health matters, and high quality day care is provided while parents attend class. "We're all working together with the child as our focus," says Barnett.

SOME FACTS ABOUT TEEN PREGNANCY

- Only half of sexually active teenagers use contraceptives the first time they have intercourse.

- About 17 percent of sexually active teenage young women report using birth control pills.

- Five out of six teenage pregnancies—nearly all—are unplanned.

- About 40 percent of teenage pregnancies end in abortion.

Trying to finish high school while also caring for a young child places heavy demands on a teenaged mother. Many find the pressure too great and drop out.

In an effort to lower the teen pregnancy rate—and also the dropout rate—some schools now offer programs teaching contraception methods.

She credits a "tremendous network of community resources" for much of the success of this program. The state sends specialists to the day care center to identify the children's needs and take early action if there are developmental problems. School nurses visit often. There is a young parents support group in Norwich, and local social services help the parents find jobs or further education. At least 75 percent of the graduates go on to more schooling or to jobs, many in the child care or health care fields. If they experience difficulties, they can return to the program for help. They can also continue to use the day care center.

Although most of the parents in the program are young women, fathers may also take part. In one case, a young father who was raising his daughter himself completed the program and received his high school diploma. He then went on to a career in the military.

Not all teen mothers drop out, and some manage to finish high school and go on to college. It takes hard work, planning, support, and motivation. Anna gets up early each day to pack her baby's diaper bag and prepare the bottles and other things she will need that day and still make it to school by 8 A.M. After a long day, she cares for the baby until her mother takes over while she goes to her part-time job at K-Mart. She comes home, tired, to more chores and her homework. The same exhausting routine begins again the next day. "It's hard, but I'm going to make it," says Anna.

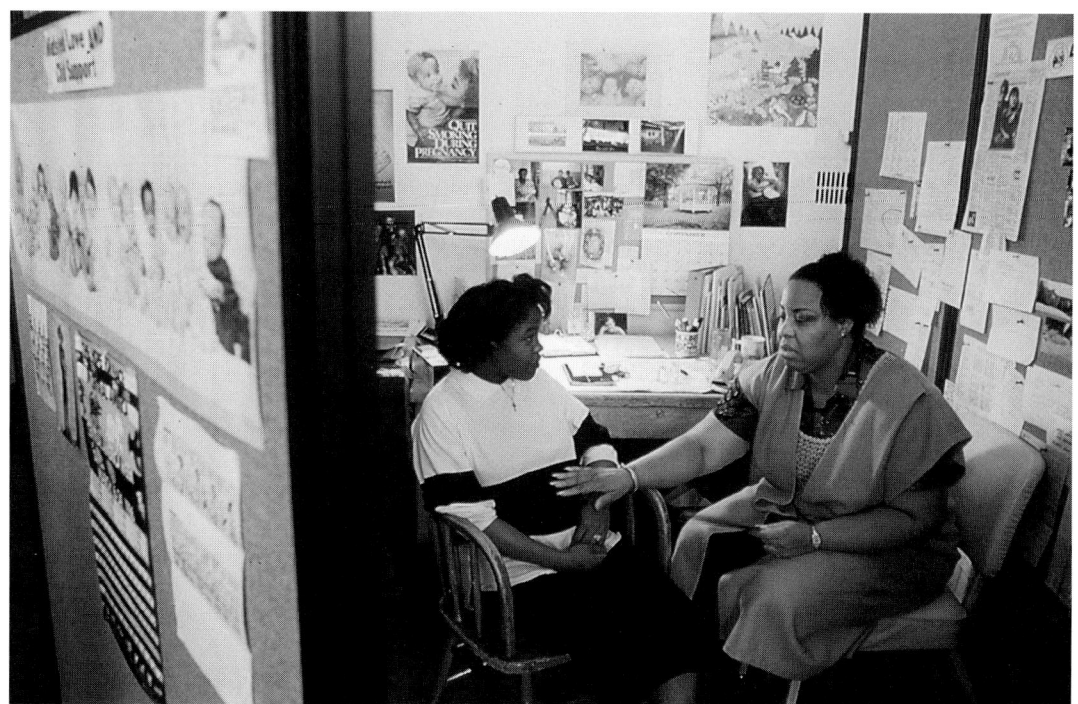

Special programs providing child care and support services can help teenaged mothers stay in school. Where these programs are available, they have been very successful.

NEGATIVE INFLUENCES

Many young people find that peer pressure leads them into drugs, gangs, and other activities that get them in trouble. Drugs and gangs are major problems in some areas and can lead young people to quit school.

Some educators call drugs the worst problem facing schools these days. Since 1990, drug use among young people has been rising. A 1994 study done by the University of Michigan shows that about 36 percent of America's high school seniors used an illegal drug that year. Students who abuse drugs or alcohol are far more likely to drop out of school than nonabusers.

In many neighborhoods, students encounter drug dealers and gang members while going to and from school, as well as in the school itself. Some teachers have said that students ask if they can linger after school, talking or helping with chores, in order to delay walking home until the gangs and dealers have gone. When they get home, some kids stay inside, where they feel a bit safer.

Schools have developed drug and alcohol education programs to warn students about the dangers of these substances. The DARE (Drug Abuse Resistance Education) program, developed and taught by law enforcement officers, is widely used. It helps students to understand and discuss the perils of using drugs and alcohol and helps them practice ways to resist peer pressure.

Even occasional or "recreational" drug use can lead to loss of motivation and poor grades. Students who abuse drugs are much more likely to drop out of school.

Some schools use undercover police and trained dogs to find illegal drugs or drug dealers. Breath tests are used to detect alcohol. Students caught using alcohol or drugs may be suspended or sent to rehabilitation programs.

Young people have been active in drug or alcohol prevention programs. Teenagers formed the group called SADD (Students Against Drunk Drivers), which educates people about this problem. Parents involved in SADD promise that they will have "safe houses"—places where alcohol is not served to teens.

SCHOOL SUPPORT GROUPS

Throughout America, hundreds of thousands of students are now taking part in support groups at school. By 1995, about half of the nation's schools were sponsoring such programs. They have sprung up in middle and elementary schools as well as high schools. At one such group, in a Chicago high school, students talk about drug or alcohol abuse by a parent, difficulties getting along with classmates, domestic violence, and various other problems.

One 15-year-old girl who attends a group for students with alcoholic parents said, "Sometimes you just want to talk and talk and talk." An Ohio teenager, who had been attending Alcoholics Anonymous meetings for his own problems, said that he found it much better to meet with people his own age.

Other students say that taking part in support groups has helped them to stay in school, get off drugs, or avoid committing crimes that might land them in jail. One 16-year-old girl quit a gang and found it easier to cope with her family problems after joining a school group. She said, "I felt that I needed to get on with my life and graduate, and it really helped that these people are not your parents."

Mike Kedzierski, the student assistance counselor at Roy C. Start High School in Toledo, Ohio, has been a leading advocate of these programs. He says that communication is vital to helping students feel respected and valued at school and to developing the resiliency they need to face their problems. "In a dysfunctional home, you can't talk, trust, or feel," says Kedzierski. "In the groups, you can. Some students just want someone to listen to them." One of his goals is to have students learn that, while they may not be able to change their circumstances or make things perfect, they will feel empowered enough to cope and change themselves.

Kedzierski is also very positive about PALS, the peer helping program at his school. There are about forty students who keep an eye out for others who may be having difficulties. The school also has mentors—staff members who "adopt" freshman students and work with them more closely. Such programs show students they are valued individuals in the school system.

4
MAKING THE MOST OF SCHOOL

I did okay in school until about a year ago. Things at home were a problem, and once I got behind, I just seemed to get more and more behind. My grades are terrible this year. I can't seem to get back on the track. Maybe I'm going to fail ninth grade, right?
—Carla, age 14

For many students, getting an education seems like a waste of time or too much work. They speak of being "bored with school" or say that their teachers and classes don't hold their interest. Many experts find this easy to understand in an age where people are used to fast-paced entertainment on television, at the movies, and in music videos. In fact, many experts blame television for creating some of the problems today's young people have in school. They say that when people grow up watching TV, they become used to the ease of watching colorful, undemanding pictures instead of learning, thinking, and concentrating. Other people blame a lack of self-discipline, motivation, or goals when students do poorly at school. Or they blame parents for not stressing school enough.

Whatever caused the problem, there is still hope. You can learn to pay attention and concentrate better. You can break the patterns that led to a dismal school experience and develop new, effective work habits.

Learning better ways to study can help improve your grades and make school seem worthwhile again.

FALLING BEHIND

It can start with little things—you skip doing homework once or twice a week, you get out of the habit of studying and find yourself doodling and daydreaming in class, you sneak off to the mall instead of school. You are unprepared whenever a teacher asks you questions about the assigned reading. You tune out of classroom discussions because you have nothing to contribute. At test time, you cram late at night in an effort to pass, then feel exhausted the next day.

Often, the less schoolwork you do, the less you feel like doing. As you get further behind, it seems more impossible than ever to catch up. Being unprepared can be quite draining. Students who keep up with their work and learn during their classes often feel more energetic after school than those who spent time and energy worrying, complaining, avoiding the work, or making excuses for missing assignments. It can be nerve-wracking to sit in class, unprepared, worrying about what will happen when the teacher asks you a question. These feelings can lead to fatigue and discouragement, again part of that downward cycle.

Another negative cycle occurs when students cheat in order to pass. They copy someone's homework or glance at another person's test. Some students

Skipping school can be the start of a downward spiral of school failure that ends in dropping out.

have resorted to copying reports word-for-word from library books because they did not want to spend the time or effort needed to do their own work.

This may solve problems in the short run—you get a better grade, the teacher isn't angry, your parents don't yell about your bad report card. But nobody can get away with cheating forever. Eventually, the lack of effort will show up. Besides, most teachers can tell when a student has done his or her own work. And those who get caught cheating not only fail the course, but are often branded as dishonest and untrustworthy for a long time.

There are many reasons why you may have gotten really behind in your schoolwork. Maybe you've been overly busy, upset over family problems, or sick. Or maybe you've just lost interest in school. Don't give up. Make appointments to work with counselors and teachers to plan a way to get back on track. They may be happy to work with you if you show them you sincerely want to catch up. You may find a way to complete parts of the work and still pass.

Try to work with your teachers, not against them. They are there to help you learn. Many are willing to meet with you after school to review material you do not understand. If you have trouble getting along with one or more teachers, find someone else at school who can help you.

CHANGING FOR THE BETTER

It might be that you could do better—even a lot better—than you are doing. Maybe you just aren't applying yourself enough. Many students who don't do well in school are bright and capable. They have more ability than their grades show. In fact, the majority of students who drop out have at least average intelligence and ability.

One major step toward doing better is to set some goals, both long-term and short-term. What do you want to accomplish? Maybe your long-term goal is to finish high school, then go on to more education or a career. A short-term goal might be to finish reading the history assignment and write the essay that was assigned for English class.

Which class do you need to work on the most? Maybe you have decided that you are going to raise your grades in one or more classes. Perhaps you are failing a subject and need to focus on that one in order to get a passing grade. While you are studying harder, you can also improve your class participation. You may decide to speak up in class at least once each day.

As you set your goals, you may have to give up some other activities that are fun but prevent you from reaching your goals. One may be watching too much television, something that many Americans do, on average, four hours or more a day. Hours spent watching "the tube" take people away from reading or active learning.

Marie Winn, author of *The Plug-In Drug*, says that watching too much television may decrease our ability to work hard and to delay gratification. Teachers also complain that students expect them to be entertainers instead of teachers. These teachers advise students to break the TV habit. Many students who have done so find that the rewards of doing well in school become more important than the temporary pleasure of watching television.

Shelly, age 16, decided that television was keeping her from doing well in school. At one point, she was watching between four and five hours each day. She decided to kick the habit gradually, substituting a half-hour of study or reading for a show that she watched Monday through Friday. She says,

> *It was reruns of a situation comedy, which I'd seen already anyway. Sitting there was just a habit. Once I cut that show, I went from a C to a B- and a B in two classes. A couple weeks later, I cut out another half-hour show, then a one-hour soap opera. I didn't really miss them. I was able to get my homework done and have time to join the field hockey team. My goal is to get down to one hour of TV on weekdays.*

LEARNING HOW TO LEARN

Better study skills may help you make the most of your study time. As many experts point out, your goal is to work *smarter*, not necessarily longer. By working smarter, you may find yourself with more free time than you expected.

To begin, it is helpful to understand how we learn. There are four basic steps in the learning process:

1. Input. We take in information through our various senses—seeing, hearing, smelling, touching, tasting. With most courses at school, you will be using your eyes and ears the most, as you read or listen to the teacher.

2. Integration. We sort out what is coming in and "file it" in our minds. That may involve putting the information in a certain order or category, organizing it, and adding it to what we already know. An example of integration is to hear a fire alarm during class and to realized that is a sign that there will be a fire drill.

3. Memory. As we receive input and and attach meaning to it, we store it in our memory for future use, obviously a major task for students in school.

4. Output. We use what has been stored to give some sort of response, whether spoken, written, or motor (body movements that show we have learned a dance step, for example).

The average teenager watches TV several hours a day. One hour less TV every day is one hour more for homework and reading.

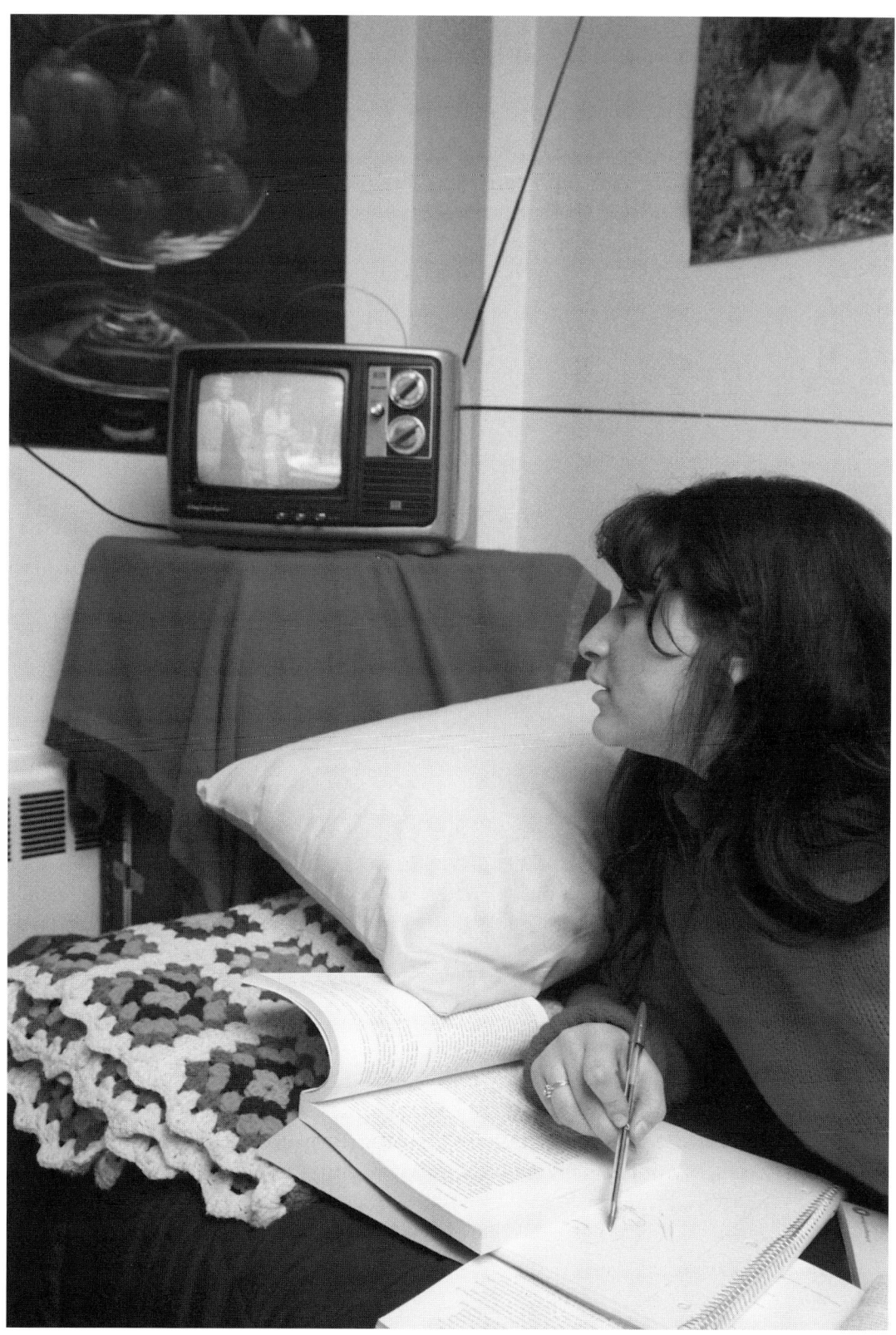

MAKING THE MOST OF SCHOOL 55

Class participation often counts toward the final grade, but some teenagers are too shy to speak up. Preparation and practice can help overcome shyness.

Looking at these steps, you can see the value of different aspects of school and studying. By listening attentively, you can maximize your input. Taking good notes can help you sort out and remember information. Reviewing study questions in a textbook can help you review what was learned and give the correct "output" when you take a test.

With these ideas in mind, educators advise us to be active learners, using more than one of our senses to take in information and remember it. This could mean reading aloud to someone, discussing what was read, making note cards for new vocabulary words, saying your spelling words into a tape recorder, or doing a science experiment as well as just hearing about it.

Are you one who speaks up during class or are you more the silent type? Speaking during class discussions may help you understand and remember the material better. Some teachers base part of your grade on class participation. By speaking up, you become more involved and may learn more.

Practice can help you overcome that shy feeling. Angie, age 14, was often too shy to speak up in class. She decided that she would contribute an idea or question at least once a day. This goal helped her to prepare better for class, since she wanted her comments to be well received. Being prepared and contributing to class discussions will also help you to see yourself as a better student. You may find yourself listening carefully to others, too.

Some schools teach students basic study skills, such as taking good notes, studying for tests, or preparing written assignments. The course is often given at the beginning of middle school or high school, when more is demanded of students.

If your school does not offer such a program but you and some other students would like one, you might ask the teachers or guidance counselor for help. Or you can form a group on your own to share ideas. You will find good books on this subject in the library. Some titles are listed at the back of this book. Time spent on these issues early on will pay off later.

ORGANIZE FOR SUCCESS

Do your weekday mornings begin pleasantly, with enough time to get dressed, eat breakfast, and gather the things you will need during the school day? Or do you dash out of bed, maybe feeling tired, throw your clothes on, and race to the bus, leaving a messy trail behind you? Do you often forget books, papers, homework, your lunch, musical instrument, or gym clothes?

When mornings follow this pattern, the day gets off to a negative start that can last till the final bell rings. All this can affect your school achievement and feelings about school in general. If you don't get enough rest or breakfast and you leave home without your homework assignment or belongings or often arrive late, you probably can't make the most of school. You may find yourself hating school, falling behind, maybe even thinking of dropping out.

Learning to organize helps many students a great deal. It can be especially helpful for students who don't like school. By organizing and planning well, you will have more time for the things you do like and still be able to finish your work.

School materials should be organized in a way that makes sense to you and improves your efficiency. If you use a backpack, try to clean it out at least once a week. Check it at night so that it will be ready to go the next day and you won't forget something in the morning rush. The same goes for lockers.

Good habits can replace the habits that cause problems. Karla, age 13, found a way to improve her situation. She often arrived at school hungry, having missed breakfast. She often forgot one or more important items, sometimes even papers and pencils. Her backpack and locker were a jumbled mess of books, papers, pencils, dirty gym clothes, gum wrappers, and other things.

Lateness, lost homework, misplaced books, and other disasters can make school a negative experience. Getting organized can help you succeed.

For a long time, Karla joked about her messy ways, calling herself a "natural-born slob." But over time, it became impossible to get through the day. Her grades slipped and she got zeros and sometimes detention for lost or forgotten homework. Her notes were so disorganized that she had a terrible time studying for tests.

Karla wanted a change. She approached a friend who had a knack for organizing things. Together, they cleaned Karla's binder, throwing out old papers and separating each subject with divider sheets. Each section contained fresh paper for notes. In the front, they put a separate sheet on which to list homework assignments. A small plastic pencil holder fit into the three-ring binder to hold pens, pencils, erasers, and a ruler. Karla got into the habit of checking this pencil holder regularly. She also began checking her alarm clock at night to make sure it was set for the right time so she would be able to eat breakfast and have time to collect the things she needed for school.

A TIME AND PLACE TO STUDY

Finding a good place to study is important. Maybe you are lucky enough to have a room of your own or a table or desk that you can use for this purpose. The ideal place is quiet and well lit, with a chair you can sit up straight in.

Perhaps things are so noisy and hectic at home that you need to find another place to study. Try the library, a church, a local YMCA or recreational center, or the home of a friend or relative, with their permission.

Set aside adequate time for studying and try to set a minimum time each day, so that you don't get behind. It's best to set those times earlier rather than too late in the evening. Be comfortable and avoid distractions. Concentrate and focus to make the most of this time. Christina, a high school sophomore, decided she wouldn't talk on the phone during her study times. When her friends called, she told them she would call back later.

Procrastination—putting off what you don't feel like doing—may be your problem. People who overcome this habit find that it feels better to get a task out of the way rather than have it hang over them, spoiling their good times. Worrying and having to make excuses to parents and teachers are the alternatives to doing the work. Take control of the task so it doesn't control you.

Some people put things off because they worry about doing them perfectly. They fear they won't meet the strict standards they have set for themselves, or that everyone else will do it better than they. Try setting a time limit for each section of the task at hand. Just aim to do a good job—it doesn't have to be perfect.

Jon, a high school freshman, had to get over his habit of procrastinating. There was always something he would rather do than study. This put him behind and caused special problems when he was sick or extra busy with sports, family events, or other activities. He decided to start with fifteen-minute study periods and add more time as he went along. As Jon became used to the new schedule, he sometimes found himself studying past the designated time because some assignments became interesting to him. As his mother and teachers began to notice his improved performance, their praise gave him another incentive to keep up his new habits.

PLANNING STUDY SESSIONS

As you look at the work you need to do each evening, make a plan. Students who get good grades suggest starting with the most difficult homework or the work that was assigned by the most demanding teachers. Take breaks as needed. Study for a certain amount of time or until you finish a chunk of work,

If you can't find a quiet, comfortable place to study at home, try the library at school or in your community.

then take a break to get a drink or snack, stretch or take a brief walk, or even nap if you are tired. Give yourself enough time, and vary the study activities to keep your mind fresh—reading, writing, note-taking, answering questions.

A lot of your study time will likely be spent doing homework assignments. Be sure to keep track of new assignments. One good way to do this is to write them down in the same place each day. If an assignment is not clear, ask questions before leaving class or school. It is also important to have the phone number of someone in each class in case you are sick or need to ask a question about homework.

Sometimes it helps to figure out why homework was assigned. Some homework helps you to practice things you are learning in class or to review what you already learned. By reviewing material when it is fresh, and on a regular basis, you can avoid having to cram before a test. Other homework teaches new things that cannot be covered during the school day.

Do your parents show an interest in your homework, even nag you about it from the minute you arrive home from school? It may seem like a pain sometimes, but having someone show interest in your schoolwork is a sign of caring about you and your future. If you find yourself arguing about homework schedules, you may need to negotiate—find times and plans that are agreeable to everyone. And once you are seen to be doing your homework on your own, the nagging will probably stop.

Be smart about time. When a project is not due for a long time, people have a tendency to relax and delay getting started. It is better to begin early, listing the steps and the materials you need, and planning partial deadlines along the way.

Should you study with a friend? Some people find that they can concentrate and stick to the task at hand, while others end up talking about other things. It takes discipline and a plan to make the most of group study sessions. Be honest with yourself. Tamara, age 14, suggests working with a schedule and starting with the material that is giving each person the most trouble.

EFFECTIVE NOTES

One way to stay involved during class and save time later on is to take good notes. To do this, you need to do more than just sit in class while the teacher talks. You need to listen actively and think about what is being discussed. Focus on the person who is speaking and try to relate what is being said to other things that you know about the subject. If you miss class for any reason, get notes from someone else.

Tanya, a high school freshman whose classmates often ask to borrow her notes, offers these tips for better note-taking:

> *I try to write neatly, even when I'm writing fast. You might think you'll remember what all your notes mean, but if they're too messy, you never will. Also, anytime teachers ask a question while talking, I write that down. Sometimes those same questions turn up on tests. And I put a star by things the teacher says more than once—that means it's pretty important. Sometimes I re-copy my notes that evening if there is a lot of material. It helps me remember things, and if something isn't clear, I can ask about it or look it up before we go on to something new.*

Taking good notes may take practice and effort, but it will pay big dividends. You will save time in the long run as you find yourself remembering more of what was said and having clear, complete notes to use when studying for tests.

If you take careful notes in class, you'll get more involved in the subject, participate more in class, and be able to study better for tests.

THE VALUE OF READING

Good readers tend to be good students. Studies show that students who enjoy reading and read at least a few hours each week have higher grades. Besides that, reading is now a part of many daily activities and jobs, whether you are trying to set up a video game, use a new kitchen appliance, understand a bus schedule, or plan a vacation. As an adult, you will have to read in order to file your income tax returns, answer mail, apply for credit cards, cook a new recipe, or read to your children.

Reading is the foundation for doing well in school. Solid reading skills are needed for finding information, comparing ideas, and understanding concepts in science, history, and other subjects. Of course, school-related reading is different than reading for pleasure. When you are reading a number of pages about a subject you find difficult or uninteresting, your mind may wander. You may find yourself turning pages without having comprehended what you "read."

One way to avoid this problem is to check yourself as you go along, asking questions about what you have read. Many textbooks have study questions for this purpose, or your teacher may ask you to read for certain information. In the long run, reading and paying attention is quicker than rereading the same pages over and over again in an inattentive way. If you are having a great deal of trouble with reading, get some help. There are many ways to teach people to read better, and people of all ages can learn to read better. If reading is a problem this year, it will only get worse as the material becomes more difficult next year.

MASTERING WRITING ASSIGNMENTS

Writing dismays many students. They dread having to turn in book reports or term papers, or even write a letter. Employers often complain that their employees have poor writing skills, even those who have high school or college diplomas. One vice president of a large American insurance company said that many of the people who apply for jobs at her company lack the writing skills to prepare a brief letter. Writing is especially important in today's world, where so many jobs require communication skills.

When a teacher assigns a writing project, it can help to break the task into smaller steps. Large tasks of any kind seem more manageable when approached one step at a time.

As you begin to put words on paper, try not to be intimidated. After all, this is a piece of paper, and you can change what you write. Even professional writers write and rewrite, revising their words many times as they go along.

Once you know a report is due, choose your topic quickly so that you can get to work. Suppose the English class assignment is to write a report about an important figure from American history and discuss that

> **STEP-BY-STEP TO A FINISHED PROJECT**
>
> You may find it helpful to break a larger task down into small steps and check off each step as it is done. For instance, suppose your assignment is to write a book report on a book about the Civil War. The steps involved are:
>
> - Go to the library
> - Choose the book
> - Read the book, one chapter at a time
> - Take notes for the report while reading
> - Organize the notes, usually in outline form
> - Write a draft
> - Revise the report
> - Write a final draft
> - Turn in your report

You need solid reading skills to do well in school. If reading is a problem for you, your school can help.

person's contribution. If you were choosing someone to write about, you would pick someone you could write about with interest. You would also want to be sure there is enough information about the person to make a solid, interesting paper.

A trip to the library comes next. Many students start by looking up their topic in an encyclopedia. This gives an overall look at the subject and may help you develop an outline. The word "outline" worries some students, but it is just another word for an organized plan. You may come up with your own ways of outlining a subject as you jot down your ideas, then put them in an order. The order will flow as you decide on your major and minor points.

Perhaps you have decided to write your report on baseball great Jackie Robinson. Your outline might cover these main topics: birth and early life; college years; marriage and graduation from UCLA; army experiences; joins Negro League Kansas City Monarchs; joins Brooklyn Dodgers as first black player in the modern major leagues; triumphs over difficulties; athletic achievements; political and business activities; death and lasting legacy. As you look at this plan, you will write topic sentences to begin each paragraph. The topic sentences give general information. Then complete each paragraph with details that elaborate on that topic.

Again, this might sound harder than it actually is. You can see this process at work in a simple thank-you letter. Suppose your grandmother sent you a new sweater for your birthday. One of the main points you will make is that you like the gift very much. Details to support this main idea might include: the color looks good on you or goes with something else you own; you like the design; this type of sweater is popular this year; you needed and can use a new sweater. So your topic sentence would be: I really like the new sweater you sent for my birthday.

TAKING TESTS

Quizzes and tests are a big part of school and one of the main ways teachers evaluate how students are doing. Many students find tests nerve-wracking. Worrying may keep them from making the most of study time or doing their best during the test itself.

In her book, *How to Take Tests,* Sara Gilbert recommends a three-step process when preparing for a test. It is called preview, view, review. Previewing means skimming—taking a look at all the material first. Viewing is working on it carefully, piece by piece. At the end, reviewing helps you check what you have learned and remember it.

Sometimes you study hard and still don't do well on a test. Maybe the questions are different from the material you learned or you misunderstood a question or two and wrote the wrong answer, even though you knew the right one. Taking tests well may require skills in addition to those you use to learn the material.

There are different kinds of tests, and different ways of preparing for them. Also, different teachers give different kinds of tests. Is your teacher heavy on names and dates? Study accordingly. You can prepare by using study questions in the book, old tests, homework that was assigned since the last test, notes taken in class, and with questions you make up on your own as you study. Flash cards may be useful for certain kinds of tests, when you have terms to define or dates and places to memorize.

Some tests—such as true/false, multiple choice, or matching questions tests—require you to recognize a correct answer and choose it from one or more wrong answers. With short answer or fill-in-the-blank tests, you have to recall and give a correct answer. Essay tests require that you recall information and express more about the subject, perhaps opinions.

Sometimes teachers give open-book tests, allowing you to bring books and possibly notes to the test. Don't make the mistake of not studying at all. Often, these tests are longer and more difficult, since you have the benefit of using your materials. You need to know basic information and how to find things

quickly. Students who rely on being able to look up everything during the test often do not finish much of the exam.

Try to get a good night's sleep and wake up in time to get ready and eat breakfast. Avoid high-sugar foods that may energize you for a short time but fizzle out later in the morning. Some protein and complex carbohydrates, such as cereal with milk and fruit, will work better.

At the test itself, try to relax as much as possible. This may be a challenge when you feel nervous. Some people take a deep breath, hold it for a count of ten, then slowly release it. Or they tighten all the muscles in their bodies, then let them relax.

Before starting, listen carefully to any spoken directions and read written directions carefully. If anything is unclear, ask. You may miss questions you know because you did not understand what the teacher wanted.

Be sure you understand whether there are penalties for guessing. In some tests, points are taken off for wrong answers, so you would avoid guessing the answers to questions you are really unsure about. Also, sometimes you have a choice of which questions to answer, for example, two out of three essay questions. Read them over, then decide which you can answer best. Find out how many points each part of the test is worth. That may help you plan how much time to spend on each section.

Lina recalls how she almost missed several questions on a test because she did not read the directions. It was a multiple-choice test, and the teacher

---

TEST-TAKING STRATEGIES

Some top students give this advice for dealing with different kinds of test questions:

"I try to answer multiple-choice questions in my head before I look at the answer choices. Sometimes one of the answers is the same as what I came up with."
—Michael, senior

"When there are different kinds of questions on a test, I look them over before answering the essays or short-answer questions. Sometimes there are words or ideas in them that I can use."
—Sheila, senior

"I show the steps in the math problems. Some teachers give you points for using the right methods, even when you come up with a wrong answer."
—Elizabeth, freshman

"I make sure I understand all the parts of an essay question, then I jot down the main points to cover. I repeat part of the question in the first sentence of my answer."
—Jack, sophomore

To get the most out of your study time, find a quiet place with no distractions and focus on the work.

Good test-taking skills can help you get better grades.

wanted the the students to mark all the answers that applied, not just one. Lina began answering the questions, trying to pick just one answer, and was quite confused until she finally went back to the beginning and saw that the directions were different from those for previous tests.

Most students allow the most time for the most difficult sections. Mitchell, age 14, also follows the time-honored rule of answering things he knows first so he will be sure to get credit for them, leaving harder questions till the end.

Machine-scored tests may intimidate people more than others. Experts urge that you follow the question numbers carefully so you are marking the right spaces as you go along.

There are books in the library that can help you deal with the many aspects of taking tests. A few of them are listed in the back of this book.

5
ALTERNATIVES TO DROPPING OUT

*Once I got into the carpentry program, school was a lot better.
I actually looked forward to each day.*
—Damian, age 16

Is it ever right to drop out of school? What if you have dropped out and want more education? Or suppose you do finish school and want a good career but don't want to go to college? What if you want to attend college but had a hard time throughout school because of learning disabilities? There are many questions to answer as you go about the important work of planning your future.

In the vast majority of cases, dropping out of school leads to many problems and limits future choices. But in some cases, for some people, dropping out may be appropriate. In their book *I Hate School: How to Hang In and When to Drop Out,* authors Claudine Wirths and Mary Bowman-Kruhm point out that there are times when it might be better for certain people to drop out of school. However, they say, you need to have a plan first. These authors, both teachers and parents, make the following suggestions.

If you are over 16 and more than two years older than most of the other students in your grade, and failing most of your classes even though you put in a good bit of time on homework and don't skip many classes, you may be better off planning a career for yourself.

If you need to work full time to help your family make enough to live on—not just to buy

Vocational training in a useful skill is one good alternative to dropping out of high school.

snacks and extras—it may be right to leave school. But don't drop out until you find a good job and have talked to your couselor about going to night school. If night school won't work, ask your school counselor about Saturday school or about taking the GED (General Educational Development) exam. This examination is administered by the American Council on Education. People who pass it receive a certificate verifying that they have "passed an exam equal to the requirements of high school." Many employers and some colleges will accept this in place of a high school diploma. In many communities, there are classes, usually held at night, to help people prepare for the GED, which is not easy to pass. The average age of those taking the test is 26.

Wirths and Bowman-Kruhm stress the importance of not dropping out until you have found a job, preferably one that will allow room to move up, helping you gain a lifelong skill so that you can support yourself comfortably.

As you think carefully about this decision, you should ask yourself some questions: Do you think you can't succeed in school? Are you just unwilling to make the effort, or don't you know how? If so, maybe you will improve your school skills and give it another try.

What if you are convinced dropping out is the only solution for you? It is important to get as much information as you can about what that means. You may know other people who have dropped out who can tell you what has happened to them since then. Where do they work? What were the advantages and disadvantages of leaving school? Are they happy with the decision they made? While you are gathering this information, make sure you don't get behind in your schoolwork in case you change your mind.

Many students find that taking a part-time job helps them to make a decision. That's what Albert did when he was considering leaving school at age 16. While working weekends as a dishwasher at a diner, he found he enjoyed the change at first. Then he began to imagine what it would be like if that were his only choice and he had to do it full time. This helped him to think more clearly about what he really wanted in the future.

Occasionally, we read about a successful actor, musician, or businessperson who dropped out of high school before graduation. While these people may have done extremely well, they are exceptions. That is why it is important to know where you are going after you leave school—to have a good plan.

It may be that you can find a job in a business run by family members or friends. This was the case with Bill, who quit school before his senior year. He became a service manager in the auto mechanics business that his grandfather had started and that his uncle had been running. Clearly, Bill had many advantages. He had grown up around this family-run business. Most dropouts would have trouble finding such a good job right away.

You may want to run a business yourself and already have the skills and resources you need to begin. This was true of Evan, who started a courier service.

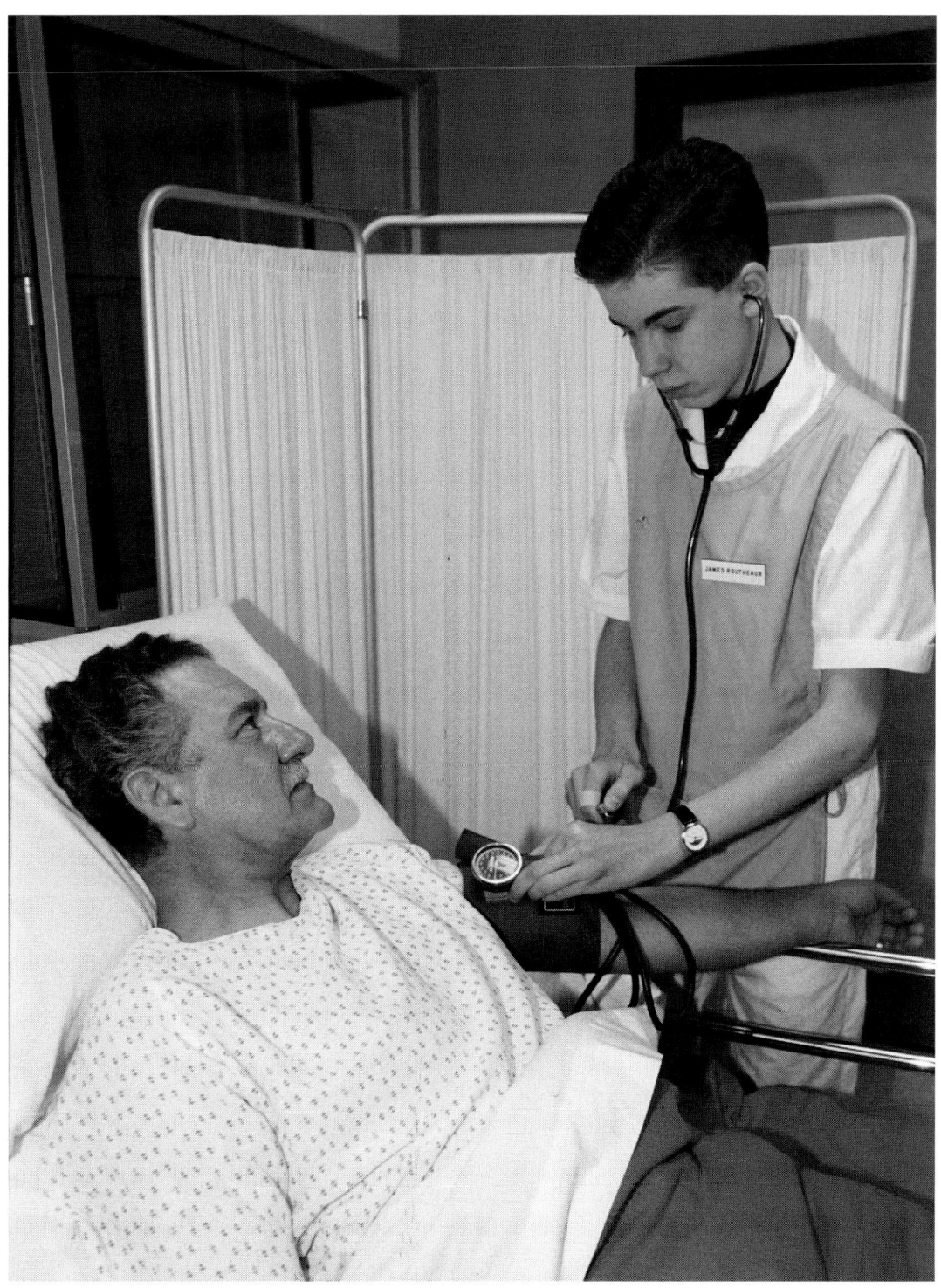

Career programs for high school students usually involve a combination of classroom work and on-the-job training.

He had seen a definite need for this type of delivery business in the region where he lived and didn't need much money or equipment to begin. In fact, he had already started the business before he dropped out of school, so he was pretty sure he could earn enough to support himself. Nonetheless, his parents were disturbed that he quit school and insisted that he attend night school and earn his diploma.

Maybe you have a particular talent that will lead to employment. Nikki hated school and never did well, but she was a great cook. One summer, she took a special cooking class run by a group of women who ran a catering service. They hired her to help bake and decorate cakes for parties. Nikki decided to drop out of school before senior year in order to work full time for this business. Through creativity and a willingness to work hard, Nikki found a job that she likes. She wants to run her own catering business someday.

VOCATIONAL TRAINING

Some students stay in school because of programs that interest them and give education more meaning. Roberto, a 17-year-old Californian, didn't like school. During his sophomore year, he cut more days than he attended. But in his junior and senior years, Roberto didn't miss a day. He and twenty-four classmates took part in a special two-year program at Berkeley High School called the Biotech Academy. The Berkeley Biotech Academy arose when Miles Inc., a health care, chemical, and imaging company, decided to expand its biotech plant in Berkeley. They decided to train low-income city residents, creating a pool of well-trained workers in the area.

Roberto's courses combine science, math, and manufacturing skills with lab work in the field of biotechnology. Roberto says he learns something meaningful every day. To help his family, Roberto also works as a dishwasher in a restaurant. He dreams of becoming a research scientist someday.

During the summer, students in this program earn money at local biotechnology companies where they serve as lab assistants or help in the field, analyzing air and water quality. They focus on practical skills and practice until they master them. They are urged to be on time and to be responsible, since real problems could occur from their negligence, as when lab animals do not receive care. Students who finish high school in this program go on to a two-year community college, after which they can apply for well-paying jobs.

One teacher at the school, Amy Hansen, described student motivation as high. Some students who had planned to drop out chose to enter this program instead and work toward a higher level career. Some enroll only in the biotech program while completing the rest of high school through a correspondence course.

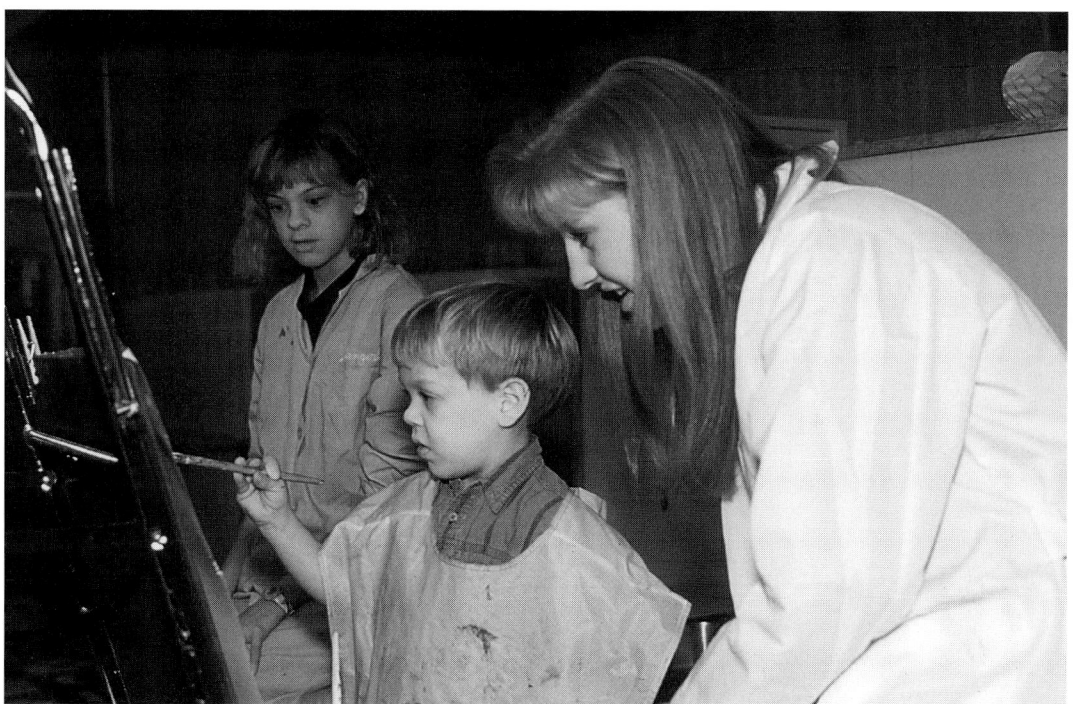

Many students see the point of school again when academic and vocational skills are taught. This young woman is being trained to work in child care.

This is one of many innovative vocational education programs that have been developed in recent years. During the early 1980s, interest in vocational education declined as educators discussed the need for higher academic standards and more rigorous courses. Vocational programs were also criticized for being so work-specific that they placed students at a disadvantage. Educators complained that many vocational programs shortchanged students and did not require enough from them. They found that some students were steered into these programs on the basis of their race or socio-economic status rather than their abilities.

As a result, vocational programs lost favor, and less emphasis was placed on them. The National Assessment of Vocational Education, done by the U.S. Department of Education, showed a declining number of students majoring in vocational subjects—from 34 percent in 1982 to 24 percent in 1992. These numbers are contining to decline.

Yet a rigid academic program may not work well for all students. Many do not plan to attend a four-year college. They learn better when combining academic and practical skills toward a particular type of job. When students see no value in school, they may begin cutting, failing, and eventually dropping out. Well-run vocational programs offer an alternative.

Experts have said that the United States lags behind other nations in this regard. Often, Americans who graduate from high school and enter the job market do not find satisfying positions until they are in their late twenties. By contrast, in Germany, most students have chosen a career between the ages of 16 and 18. About 60 percent of students begin working and receiving training at regular jobs while they attend high school. There are more programs linking school and jobs in Germany, Japan, and other industrialized nations. Lester Thurow, a well-known American economist and author, has said, "The United States is unique among industrial countries in that it does not have an organized post-secondary education system for the non-college-bound."

The federal government approved grants to improve vocational education programs in its 1994 School-to-Work Opportunities Act. This act will increase the number of apprenticeships and other work-based programs all over America. It provides for creative new ways of developing the "school-to-work" approach.

Programs are changing to keep up with today's jobs. At one time, woodworking, auto mechanics, bookkeeping, and secretarial skills were among the few programs available. Today, there are many more choices. In Philadelphia, students can attend a high school that focuses on specific jobs, such as the Academy for Fitness, Health Promotion and Sports Education, or the Hotel, Restaurant, and Tourism Academy. All over America, these kinds of academies prepare people for careers in aviation, health, electrical trades, interior design, landscaping, accounting, marketing, and other fields.

Richard C. Burley, the director of a three-school vocational technical program in Pennsylvania, says that there are jobs in certain fields waiting for qualified applicants, including diesel mechanics, computer repair people, welders, machinists, electricians, masons, and refrigeration workers. Besides the vocational training for specific jobs, college-bound students come to this program for courses that will help them in their fields later on.

In Lancaster, Pennsylvania, students who have received training in carpentry, masonry, or electrical wiring use their skills to build homes ranging in price from $150,000 to $200,000. Teachers in this program place students in situations that are like those they will face on the job.

In Rothsay, Minnesota, students have learned to run a lumber yard, hardware store, or grocery by taking over businesses that had failed or closed down. They earn credits for managing these businesses and doing accounting, marketing, and other tasks. In addition, students have learned how to apply for bank loans and federal grants. As of 1994, the dropout rate at this school was zero. Tom Fossy, a teacher and businessman who helped to develop this project, said, "What the business world wants is people who are creative, who are problem-solvers and lifelong learners; in school, we call those people disrup-

Vocational programs change to keep pace with changes in the job market. Many high schools now offer training in computer operations and technology.

tive." He believes that by working cooperatively together in a real-life situation, students become well prepared for today's workforce.

Says Kenneth Gray, a professor of education at Pennsylvania State University, "Most policy makers seriously underestimate the number of students who want to go to work right after graduation. . . . We need to help students see that there are ways to win other than aspiring to a four-year degree and turning into a lawyer."

Some high schools offer apprenticeships in which students begin learning and working in high school, then continue this process for two years in junior college. These are run in connection with local businesses and sometimes labor unions.

The Rindge School of Technical Arts in Cambridge, Massachusetts, uses a multifaceted approach to learning that broadens students' opportunities after graduation. There is strong academic content as well as hands-on learning and practical applications. For example, in the "Cityworks" program, ninth-graders spend the year exploring the city, making complex maps, taking photos, interviewing residents, and learning the history of the town from oral and written sources. Students in the carpentry course study environmental issues, such as deforestation and zoning, as well as doing technical work. Larry Rosenstock, executive director of the Rindge School, says that students bring a lot of energy to these courses and "feel like they're doing adult work."

Students who complete well-run technical programs have many options for jobs or further education. Some choose to attend college. Graduates of the Chicago High School for Agricultural Sciences find that their preparation in the sciences, especially biology, gives them a head start as science majors. Some have gone on to medical school. Students who have enjoyed learning at vocational-technical high schools like the chance to learn while earning money. Some also found the teachers to be especially supportive. "It was the best combination for me—I got a diploma, so I have many choices about the future. And I have a career I can pursue right now," says one graduate.

RETURNING TO SCHOOL

Mike is an example of someone who left school, then found a reason to return. As part of a rock band that played at local dances, Mike thought he might have a career as a musician. He dropped out in order to write music and record a "demo" with his band. The demo did not sell, and the band fell apart after two members left.

In the meantime, Mike met someone who steered him to a job touring with an established musical group as a "roadie"—someone who helps to set up the equipment that moves with the band from concert to concert. While on this tour, Mike realized that he had a talent for sound engineering. He loved watching the sound man on the tour operate the board of complex switches that balanced the vocals and different instruments during the concert. As he learned more about this field, Mike found that his best bet was to receive technical training through a junior college program. As a result, he returned to school, with the goal of graduating, then enrolled in a two-year college program to pursue his chosen career.

Some people return to school at the urging of employers. Employers have complained that many of their entry-level workers are not well prepared, even though they did graduate from high school. Today's workplaces demand a higher level of skills than ever before. Corporations spend millions of dollars each year on remedial education programs for workers.

Discouraged by the kinds of jobs they get, some people who drop out of school later return or seek adult education and job training. Some who lack basic skills in reading find help in adult literacy programs or adult education programs run by the community.

It is estimated that about 3 percent of all Americans cannot read at all. Some dropped out of high school, but others managed to graduate, having been

No matter when you drop out of school, you can always go back. Community-based literacy programs help anyone who asks.

ALTERNATIVES TO DROPPING OUT 79

passed from grade to grade, without gaining this basic skill. About 20 percent of all Americans are not reading at the eighth-grade literacy level, which is the level needed in many jobs today. Some 5 percent of Americans read below the fourth-grade level.

There are more than 20,000 community-based literacy programs in America to help people gain reading skills. However, many people do not stay in the programs very long. A study done by the COSMOS Corporation, a Washington, D.C., public policy research group, found that about half of the people who enroll in adult literacy programs drop out before completing them. Most drop out within a few weeks of starting a program. Another study showed even higher rates—70 to 80 percent. People said that they left because they lacked transportation or day care for children or because the program did not suit their needs. A common complaint was that the program moved too fast and they could not keep up.

At the Mercy Learning Center in Bridgeport, Connecticut, the Sisters of Mercy help adult women learn to read. Sister Eileen Boffa, a former principal with a master's degree in urban education, was one of the founders of the center. She says, "Our philosophy is that when you teach a mother, you teach a whole family." At the center, she and other staff members and volunteers develop individualized plans for each student. They use both one-on-one teaching and intensive study classes for those whose reading skills are at least fourth-grade level.

When they began the program in 1987, they went to housing projects and other places to invite people to come to the center. Many of their students have experienced school failure and a number had dropped out of high school. There were also language barriers, since a number of students were Spanish-speaking, with English as their second language.

By 1995, the center was serving about 100 women. Among their success stories is a Latino woman who began without knowing how to read or even recognize many letters of the alphabet. For months, she worked hard with a tutor. When she did finally learn to read, her 16-year-old daughter asked her mother to read her a story, something she had longed for since she was a child. It was a joyous moment for their family.

Another woman, Maria, came to the center in her mid-thirties, reading at the third-grade level. Her dream was to earn her GED. After working hard to improve her reading, writing, and math skills, Maria entered the GED program, where she worked very hard, at the same time studying with a tutor at the Mercy Center. Eventually, she earned a child development degree at a community college while working at full-time and rearing two sons. Mother and sons often did their homework together.

There are many programs for adult learners. It is never too late to learn new skills or improve old ones. People can return to the education system throughout their lives, as well as continue to learn on their own.

The difference between school success and dropping out is often the interest of just one teacher who cares.

HELPING STUDENTS SUCCEED

"I was on the verge of dropping out," recalls Juan, now in his twenties. "I had made up my mind when I turned 16 that I was out of here." What changed Juan's mind? A teacher took a special interest in him. She gave him extra help after school and kept encouraging him, saying "I know you have it in you."

As experts study America's schools and work to improve public education, they find that many students need what Juan found at his school: someone to care about him and his future, someone to convince him he could succeed. There are other things schools are doing to help more students achieve their potential and leave school better prepared for adult life.

The nation as a whole benefits when people are well educated and productive. The economy thrives when people can afford to buy goods and services and pay taxes. For these and other reasons, the states and the federal government have been working to reduce dropout rates. One of their goals is to improve schools so that students have the resources they need to reach their potential.

In 1983, the Department of Education discussed problems in public education in a widely-publicized book called *A Nation At Risk*. Six years later, President George Bush met with all fifty of the nation's governors in Charlottesville, Virginia, to discuss ways to improve education. This education summit, as it was called, was only the third time in history that a president has called such a meeting with governors. (The first was convened in 1908 by President Theodore Roosevelt and focused on conservation; the second, called by President Franklin Roosevelt in 1933, addressed the problems of the Great Depression.)

At the 1989 meeting, the president and the governors developed new education goals for America. One important goal was to reduce the dropout rate to no more than 10 percent by the year 2000. Many suggestions were made about reaching that goal, and some of these ideas have led to successful programs. You may be involved in such programs yourself, or they may someday affect your children. As citizens, future voters, taxpayers, and parents, it is important to understand what is going on in education, since it can affect all of us in some way.

LOWERING THE DROPOUT RATE

SIX MAJOR STRATEGIES

1. Intervene early for problems, in the preschool and early school years

2. Create a positive school climate

3. Set high expectations

4. Select and develop strong teachers

5. Provide a broad range of instructional programs

6. Initiate collaborative efforts

—from the Urban Superintendents Network, 1987

SCHOOL REFORMS

During the 1980s and 1990s, some experts said that instead of looking at what was wrong with students who drop out, we should look more closely at what is wrong with schools and how they could be better. Schools can be made more personal, welcoming, and meaningful to students, say these educators.

Large urban schools have come in for special criticism. Jeanne Frankl, executive director of the Public Education Association, has called some of them "large, anonymous, and boring," saying that students often feel put off by the atmosphere at such schools. They may feel alienated and unimportant rather than part of a community.

One Los Angeles student attended a large school and was planning to drop out when he was sent to Odyssey High School, which has special programs for young people at risk for school failure and discipline problems. At graduation, he said that until he came to Odyssey, he felt "like a nobody. . . . Odyssey is not just a high school; it's a family. A family loves and cares for one another, and that's what Odyssey does. . . . They never gave up on me; they stood behind me all the way."

Some large schools have set up smaller schools within large buildings so that students can feel more comfortable and get to know a smaller group of teachers well. Other programs assign a teacher to follow each student's progress, making home visits and meeting with the student on a regular basis. Older students may be assigned to befriend younger ones.

Schools also work to increase parental involvement, since that is another factor that tends to create a more friendly feeling in the community and increase school achievement. Dr. James P. Comer, a psychiatrist at Yale University, developed a successful program in New Haven, Connecticut, that brings parents into schools. "I began to think about how you could make a difference for low-income kids, and I decided that the only place you could in our society—because you

Small programs within or instead of a large, anonymous high school often help students who feel lost or turned off by school. Here, students at one such alternative high school raise money for their program with a car wash.

can't get to families earlier—is the school," he says. The Comer method helps parents, teachers, and students to work together on mutual goals, in a supportive environment. Schools that have tried this method found that students' behavior problems were reduced, while their test scores went up.

Other school reforms have focused on how schools are funded. In some states, there have been great differences in the amount of money for some schools as opposed to others. To narrow such differences, some states have devised new ways of collecting money and distributing it to schools. Some states have passed laws to ensure that poor districts will have adequate funding.

Another issue in the news is "school choice." Some people would like the government to give parents education vouchers—certificates worth a certain amount of money. These could be used to pay for education at any private or public school, depending on the parent's choice. Supporters of this idea say that it would improve schools by making them more competitive. Critics say that choice plans would be difficult to implement if too many people chose the same school. They also fear there might be more segregation by race, income, or ethnic background.

HELPING STUDENTS AT RISK

Some groups of students are at special risk of school failure and dropping out. They may face many problems and disadvantages in trying to get an education. These include members of minority groups—African Americans, Latinos, Native Americans—and children of migrant farmworkers. Young people in these groups often must deal with poverty, as well as racism and other problems. When given the same opportunities as other students, they show the same range of abilities and achievement.

In the past, dropout rates among Native Americans have been about twice as high as those in the general population. Less than 10 percent of all Native Americans held college degrees by 1990. Native Americans have suffered from severe economic problems. Health problems, unemployment, shorter life expectancies, malnutrition, and other problems have followed.

In 1967, a special government committee report expressed shock at the inadequate schools that were found in Indian reservation areas: "Our national policies . . . have not offered Indian children—either in years past or today—an educational opportunity anywhere near equal to that offered the great bulk of American children."

Among the changes the committee recommended was more Indian control over their school systems. In recent years, tribal groups have developed programs that combine standard courses with studies of Native American cultures and languages. More Native Americans have been going on to higher education.

Migrant farmworkers experience high dropout rates, too—about 50 percent before students reach ninth grade. Only 11 to 12 percent of migrant teens enter the twelfth grade, according to statistics from the U.S. Department of Health and Human Services. Migrants contend with health problems, language barriers, and poverty. They frequently move about, changing jobs and schools. Yet many families value education and are quick to enroll their children in the nearest school as soon as they relocate for work.

A federally funded program called the Migrant Education Fund has tried to help young people. Its dropout-prevention program offers literacy and English classes and tutoring. Parents are encouraged to become involved. Thousands of migrant children live near Santa Cruz, California, where a program called *Yo Puedo* (I Can) is available. Migrant high school students involved in *Yo Puedo* can attend a summer program at the University of California campus in Santa Cruz. They attend classes all day and work with teachers in the evening. Besides academic classes, they take part in leadership training, cultural enrichment activities, and communication skill groups. Again, parents are often included.

Yo Puedo students often go on to colleges and universities after high school. Eugenia Ortiz, who attended this program, said, "It builds confidence and gives us the motivation to continue our education."

Many educators believe the best way to help students who are at risk of school failure is to provide strong early childhood education. Although studies have shown the value of Head Start and other pre-school programs that serve disadvantaged children, there is not enough federal funding of such programs to accommodate all those who are eligible. In early 1990, only one of every five children who qualified could be served. Some citizens hope that Congress will eventually make early childhood education a national priority, since it may be an investment in the future. Spending money on health care and pre-school programs for very young children could prevent higher costs later on.

A number of people point out that that a child's early life has a strong influence on later school achievement. "How well a child does in school depends on the child-care system in the five years before school," says Dr. Edward Zigler. Zigler helped to found the Head Start program during the 1960s and went on to become director of the Bush Center for Child Development and Social Policy at Yale University. He sees the three major influences on children today as family, school, and the child-care system, and worries that between 3 and 5 million kids are latch-key children going home to empty houses. "Children should not be alone at home," he says. "They should be in the care of adults."

Businessman Eugene Lang is the founder of the I Have a Dream Foundation. This organization provides incentives and assistance to help young people stay in school and graduate.

COMMUNITY INVOLVEMENT

With so many needs to meet, schools are looking to the outside community and to business leaders for help. A number of individuals and groups work with schools to help students succeed. Adult volunteers work in schools as aides, library assistants, and hall monitors. Young people help by tutoring younger children. One 13-year-old who takes part in weekly reading and writing sessions with a 9-year-old girl in a special-education class says, "We have a good time. I always look forward to Fridays. It's nice being the teacher for a change."

In some cities, local corporations have sponsored schools. Employees have become mentors and tutors at the schools, and the companies have paid for equipment that the schools or students needed. Large corporations have also funded grants for experimental programs that aim to reduce high dropout rates.

Millionaire businessman Eugene Lang started a program that has given many young people an incentive to finish high school. In 1981, he visited the New York City neighborhood where he had grown up. At Public School 121, Lang addressed the graduating sixth-graders and told them that if they finished high school, he would pay for their college educations.

Lang set up the I Have a Dream Foundation (IHAD) to distribute money donated by corporations and individuals who want to help students throughout America reach their dream of college. Many of the IHAD students overcome obstacles to finish school. Besides contributing money, sponsors in the program become personally involved with students. Lang says, "You have to keep reinvigorating them, rekindling their ambition, helping them overcome problems—which may be emotional, economic, sociological." Kevin, who became part of IHAD at age 15, has been keeping his grades up while working part-time at a restaurant. "I used to think I couldn't make it," he says. "Now I think I can." The mother of another "dreamer" says, "It opens doors. We have great hopes."

LOOKING TOWARD THE FUTURE

To many people, giving young people a dream for the future and something to hope for is the most important way to help them reach their potential, both in school and out. Says Les Brown, the well-known author and motivational speaker, "We must nurture our kids early on and give them a vision of themselves in the future, because if you can't see how you fit into the future, you will act like a misfit, and things like education and self-enrichment won't have any value to you. You become angry and bitter at the world and mostly at yourself."

Dr. James P. Comer might easily have been a school dropout instead of a well-known physician and Associate Dean of the Yale School of Medicine. Dr.

Comer grew up poor and black in East Chicago, Indiana. But his mother, Maggie, who did not even finish first grade, was determined that her five children would not only finish school, but also college. As a domestic worker, Mrs. Comer watched closely how middle-class families enhanced their children's education. The Comer family went to the library and visited museums and attended educational events. Mrs. Comer kept in touch with teachers and made sure that homework assignments were done.

Dr. Comer recalls that his friends were also bright and able, but many "went on a downhill course." Their parents did not know how to help them, and the schools did not understand their lifestyles and problems. The Comer children went on to graduate from college and receive advanced degrees. Dr. Comer was graduated from medical school, became a child psychiatrist, and developed an effective program to improve public schools in New Haven, Connecticut. It has become a model for school reform in other places as well.

Joseph A. Fernandez, former superintendent of schools in both Miami, Florida, and New York City, was himself once a school dropout. Fernandez grew up in Harlem, a low-income section of New York, and quit high school before graduating. Later he joined the Air Force and earned a high school equivalency diploma. After leaving the Air Force, he studied at Columbia University, then at the University of Miami. After graduating, he became a mathematics teacher. Fernandez continued to advance in his profession. As a superintendent in Miami, he developed a program that reduced the dropout rate in that city. Dr. Fernandez believes that his story shows how hard work and a desire to learn can help people overcome their early problems.

Often, dreams of a better future have kept people going in spite of adversity. Regardless of what other people are doing, you still have choices about what you want to do. You can choose to set a different goal and make the most of your education and talents.

Alternative programs such as City Year in New York City give high school students a chance to perform meaningful service—and get paid for it.

ADDITIONAL RESOURCES

Phone Numbers to call:
800 numbers are toll-free calls. There is no charge for calling a telephone number that begins with 1-800.

AL-ANON and Alateen
1-800-356-9996
(Support groups for the family members of alcoholics)

Alcohol and Drug Help
1-800-821-HELP

Cocaine Hotline
1-800- COCAINE

Contact Literacy Hotline
1-800-228-8813
1-800-552-9097

Equal Employment Opportunity Commission
1-800-669-4000

"Just Say No" International
1-800-258-2766
(In California: 1-415-939-6666)

National GED Info Hotline
1-800-626-9433
1-800-552-9097

National Domestic Violence Hotline
1-800-333-7233

Problem Pregnancy Hotline
1-800-228-0332

Runaway's Hotline
1-800-231-6946
1-800-392-3352

Organizations you can write to or call:

Academic Therapy Publications
20 Commercial Blvd.
Novato, CA 94949
(800) 422-7249
Publishes *Directory of Facilities and Services for the Learning Disabled.*

American Vocational Association
1410 King Street
Alexandria, VA 22314
(800) 826-9972

Aspira Association
1112 16th Street NW, Suite 340
Washington, DC 20036
(202) 835-3600
This group helps Latino youth stay in school.

Association for Community Based Education
1805 Florida Avenue NW
Washington, DC 20009
(202) 462-6333
An organization for adult literacy.

Association of Learning Disabled Adults
P.O. Box 9722
Friendship Station
Washington, DC 20016
(301) 593-1035

Center to Prevent Handgun Violence
1225 Eye St. NW, Suite 1100
Washington, D.C. 20005
(202) 289-7319

CHADD (Children with Attention Deficit Disorder)
499 NW 70th Avenue, Suite 308
Plantation, FL 33317
(305) 587-3700

Council for Exceptional Children (CEC)
1920 Association Drive
Reston, VA 22091
(703) 620-3660

Foundation for Children With Learning Disabilities (FCLD)
99 Park Ave
New York, NY 10016
(212) 586-2464

Learning Disabilities Association of America (LDA)
4156 Library Road
Pittsburgh, PA 15234
(412) 341-1515

Male Youth Enhancement Project
1510 9th Street NW
Washington, DC 20001
(202) 332-0213

Martin Luther King Center for Nonviolent Social Change
449 Auburn Ave. NE
Atlanta, Georgia 30312
(404) 524-1956

National Assault Prevention Center
P.O. Box 02005
Columbus, Ohio 43202
(614) 291-2540

National Center for Learning Disabilities, Inc. (NCLD)
99 Park Avenue
New York, NY 10016
(212) 687-7211

National Coalition of Advocates for Students
100 Boylston Street
Boston, MA 02167
(617) 357-8507

National Dropout Prevention Center
205 Martin Street
Clemson University
Clemson, SC 29634
(803) 656-2599

National School Safety Center
4165 Thousand Oaks Boulevard, Suite 290
Westlake Village, CA 91362
(805) 373-9977

Orton Dyslexia Society
Chester Building, Suite 382
Baltimore, MD 21286
(410) 296-0232

Resolving Conflict Creatively
163 Third Avenue, Suite 239
New York, New York 10009
(212) 260-6290

FOR FURTHER READING

Benjamin, Robert. *Making Schools Work: A Reporter's Journey Through Some of America's Most Remarkable Classrooms.* New York: Continuum Publishing Corporation, 1981.

Boyer, Ernest. *High School: A Report on Secondary Education in America.* New York: Harper and Row, 1983.

Brutten, Milton. *Something's Wrong With My Child.* New York: Harcourt Brace Jovanovich, 1973.

Colligan, Louise, and Doug Colligan. *The A Plus Guide to Good Grades.* New York: Scholastic Book Services, 1979.

Fisher, Gary L. and Rhoda Woods Cummings. *The Survival Guide for Kids With LD* (Learning Differences).* Minneapolis: Free Spirit, 1990.

Fry, Ronald W. *How to Study.* Hawthorne, N.J.: The Career Press, 1989.

Gilbert, Susan. *How to Take Tests.* New York: William Morrow, 1983.

Goodlad, John. *A Place Called School: Prospects for the Future.* Hightstown, NJ: McGraw-Hill, 1983.

Hall, David E. *Living With Learning Disabilities: A Guide For Students.* Minneapolis: Lerner Publications, 1993.

Kaufman, G. and L. Raphael. *Stick Up for Yourself! Every Kid's Guide to Personal Power and Self-Esteem.* Minneapolis: Free Spirit, 1990.

Kidder, Tracy. *Among Schoolchildren.* Boston: Houghton-Mifflin, 1989.

Knox, Jean McBee. *Learning Disabilities.* New York: Chelsea House, 1989.

Levine, Mel. *Keeping A Head In School: A Student's Book about Learning Abilities and Disabilities.* Cambridge, MA: Educators Publishing Service, 1990.

Maeroff, Gene. *Don't Blame the Kids: The Problem With America's Public Schools.* New York: McGraw-Hill, 1982.

Mangrum, Charles T. and Stephen S. Strichert. *Peterson's Guide to Colleges with Programs for Learning Disabled Students.*

Marek, M. *Different, Not Dumb.* New York: Franklin Watts, 1986.

National Coalition of Advocates for Children. *Barriers to Excellence: Our Children At Risk.* Boston: National Coalition of Advocates for Children (NCAC), 1985.

Oakes, Jeannie and Martin Lipton. *Making the Best of Schools: A Handbook for Parents, Teachers, and Policymakers.* New Haven: Yale University Press, 1990.

Ravitch, Diane. *The Schools We Deserve: Reflections on the Educational Crises of Our Times.* New York: Basic Books, 1985.

Rosner, Jerome. *Helping Children Overcome Learning Difficulties.* New York: Walker, 1975.

Wesson, McClenahan Carolyn. *Teen Troubles: How to Keep Them From Becoming Tragedies.* New York: Walker, 1988.

Wirths, Claudine and Mary Bowman-Kruhm. *I Hate School: How to Hang In and When to Drop Out.*

Glossary

Attention deficit disorder. A condition characterized by difficulty focusing and sustaining attention.

Auditory memory. Ability to remember what is heard.

Dyslexia. A disturbance in the ability to read.

GED (general educational development). A certification that someone has passed a test roughly equivalent to the requirements of high school.

Hyperactivity. A neurological condition characterized by excessive motor activity.

Learning disability. A disorder of one or more of the basic psychological processes involved in understanding and using language, spoken or written, which may manifest itself in an imperfect ability to listen, think, speak, read, write, spell or do mathematical calculations.

Literacy. Ability to read.

Mainstream. Regular education classes as opposed to special education classes.

Mediate. Help to settle disputes.

Neurologist. Doctor who deals with problems of the nervous system.

Resource room. Place where a learning specialist delivers specialized teaching to one or more students.

Sequencing. The ability to do things in order or in logical steps.

Visual discrimination. The ability to see differences among various shapes, numbers, and letters.

Visual processing. The ability to perceive information that comes in through the eyes.

Vouchers. Certificates worth a certain amount of money that could be used to pay tuition at the school of one's choice.

INDEX

A

adult education, 28, 80
alcohol abuse, 12-13, 36, 47-48
American Council on Education, 31, 72
attention deficit disorder (ADD), 20-21

B

Barnett, Janet, 44-45
Berkeley Biotech Academy, 74
Boffa, Sister Eileen, 80
Bowman-Kruhm, Mary, 71-72
Brown, Les, 87
Burley, Richard C., 76
Bush, Barbara, 20
Bush, George, 82

C

Carnegie Foundation, 36
cheating, 52-53
Cher, 20
child abuse, 36
Chrysler Corporation, 9
Clark, Joe, 41
class participation, 53, 56-57
Comer, Dr. James P., 83-84, 87-89
community colleges, 30
conflict mediation programs, 43
COSMOS Corporation, 80
counseling programs, 15
crime rates, 10, 25
Cruise, Tom, 20

D

DARE program, 47
Department of Commerce, 10
Department of Education, 7, 13, 44, 75, 82
Department of Health and Human Services, 85
Dropping out
    crime and, 10, 25
    learning disabilities and, 25
    poor grades and, 11-12
    poverty and, 12
    pregnancy and, 12, 43-46
    reducing, 82
    statistics on, 7-8, 25
drug abuse, 12-13, 36 47-48
dyslexia, 20, 26

E

Edison, Thomas A., 30
emotional problems, 35-36
Education Network, 12
Education of All Handicapped Children Act, 28
Einstein, Albert, 30

F

Family Life Development Center, 43
Federal Bureau of Investigation, 41
Fernandez, Joseph A., 89
Fossy, Tom, 76-77
Frankl, Jeanne, 82

G

gangs, 42
Garbarino, James, 43
GED exam, 72, 80
Gilbert, Sara, 65
grades, 11-12
GRADS program, 44
Gray, Kenneth, 77
Gwaltney, Gene, 9

H

Hallowell, Edward M., 20-21
health levels, 10, 85
Head Start program, 85
Holmes, Laurie, 12
homelessness, 38-40
homework, 60-61

I

Iacocca, Lee, 9
I Have a Dream Foundation, 87
Individuals with Disabilities Acts, 28

J

Jenner, Bruce, 20
job training, 15
junior colleges, 30

K

Kearns, David, 11
Kedzierski, Mike, 49

L

Lang, Eugene, 86, 87
language barriers, 12, 80, 85
learning disabilities, 15, 17-18, 71. See also attention deficit disorder; dyslexia.
    causes of, 21-22
    college programs for, 30-33
    help for, 27-29
    identifying, 25-27
    occurrence of, 21
    problems from, 22-25
    specific, 18-21
literacy programs, 28, 79-80

M

Mangrum, Charles T., 30
McDonald's Corporation, 9
Mercy Learning Center, 80
Migrant Education fund, 85
military service, 10

N

National Assessment of Vocational Education, 75
National Center for Children and Youth, 28
National Institute of Mental Health, 22
National School Safety Center, 41
Native Americans, 84-85
night school, 72
Norwich Free Academy, 44-45
note-taking skills, 61

O

Odyssey High School, 83
organizing skills, 57-58

P

PALS program, 49
parental neglect, 12, 36, 37-38
peer counseling, 48-49
peer pressure, 13, 47
poverty, 12, 36-37
pregnancy, 12, 43-46
    programs
    statistics on, 44
procrastinating, 59
Public Education Association, 82

Q

Quinn, Terrence, 39

R

reading skills, 62-63
Riley, Richard W., 8
Rindge School of Technical Arts, 77-78
Russell Corporation, 9

S

SADD program, 48
Savage, John F., 24
Scholastic Aptitude Test (SAT), 31-32
school reforms, 82-84
School-to-Work Opportunities Act, 76
Smith, Sally L., 22, 30
special education programs, 29
Stein, Stan, 9
Stewart McKinney Homeless Assistance Act, 39
Strichert, Stephen S., 30
study skills, 52-53
    improving, 54-57, 59-61
support groups, 38, 44, 48-49

T

Teens on Target program, 43
television watching, 51, 53-54
test-taking skills, 65-69
Thurow, Lester, 76
tutoring programs, 15

U

University of Michigan, 47

V

violence, 13, 15, 40-43
    statistics on, 40
vocational rehabilitation programs, 28
vocational education programs, 74-78

W

Widom, Cathy Spatz, 36
Winn, Marie, 54
Wirths, Claudine, 71-72
writing skills, 63-65

X

Xerox Corporation, 11

Y

Yo Puedo program, 85